Distortion of Islam

Also by Anor Azhak…

Ignorance and Violence: Quest for the Truth. Canada:
Trafford Publishing, 2001.

Distortion of Islam

by

Anor Azhak

Printed in Victoria, BC, Canada.

ISBN: 978-1-4269-1854-4 (soft)
ISBN: 978-1-4269-1855-1 (hard)

Library of Congress Control Number: 2009938679

*Our mission is to efficiently provide the world's finest, most comprehensive book publishing
service, enabling every author to experience success. To find out how to publish your
book, your way, and have it available worldwide, visit us online at www.trafford.com*

Trafford rev. 11/16/2009

 www.trafford.com

North America & international
toll-free: 1 888 232 4444 (USA & Canada)
phone: 250 383 6864 ♦ fax: 812 355 4082

Table of Contents

DEDICATION

Since America and Europe are the children, or grandchildren, of their progenitor Asia; and since neither of them has had the chance to realize the reality about the religion of Muhammad or the religion of Jesus, peace be upon them, I dedicate the present book to them.

FOREWORD

IN THE NAME OF ALLAH, THE
COMPASSIONATE, THE MERCIFUL

When it dawned on me that freedom lies behind the bars of
ignorance that we ourselves have built, I felt it was my duty to
write the present book.

PREFACE

Why is it that the Muslim World is so backward? Why is it that life expectancy in our part of the world is short in contrast with the West and Japan, and why is it that our average income is much lower than in the affluent nations? And why does not the Muslim World surprise the rest of the world with any forward leaps? It was such questions that were posed by a distinguished Muslim thinker, Jawdat Sa'eed.

The situation is even graver when we consider the extorted territories, the grabbed wealth, the cheaply spilled blood, the absent justice under tyrants supported by the big powers, the ill-informed clerics, and the deep darkness of ignorance to which the masses cling tightly, yet brag of being a Muslim community.

Here you find a human being who has been stripped of the essence of his humanity; he is called 'a subject', and he has been deprived of his political freedom, and of his civil rights; he is virtually in a prison where he has neither intellectual nor moral freedom; and on top of that he is continually reminded of the favor of letting him enjoy an abject and servile life.

Such solutions as are suggested for the crises seem to worsen them rather than solve them; it is hence no wonder that every thinking person asks, "Is the problem in the thinkers, or in our dire conditions?" Some have gone so far as to wonder if the basic thought is defective.

By looking carefully and attentively, by an analytical study of such slogans as prevail among Muslims on the one hand, and by considering the contradictory utterances of clerics on the other hand, one will realize quite evidently to what extent the Muslims have gone astray: there is no consensus on the causes of the Islamic dilemma, not to mention the right solutions. Some blame the agony of the Muslim World on the West, on colonialism or foreign dominance or imperialism; others would say that Islamic thinking must be updated to pick up with the current realities; a third group suggests that the solution must be in political Islam, that the absence of Islam from the political arena is the cause of our failure. The diversity of explanations must cause an observer to feel quite dizzy: some would theorize on the debate of religions, others attach their hope to violence, and between the two extremes are a plethora of trends. It is enough for an observer just to watch the crazy talks relayed on TV channels in weekly programs, claiming to be the right approach to 'religion and life'. No wonder that, in the minds of most outsiders, Islam and terrorism have become synonymous.

We must conclude that the conflicts we witness in the approaches, ennobled with such designations as 'opinion and counter-opinion', are in reality a single self-contradictory opinion, a form of delusion that has nothing to do with the light of knowledge. What we witness is pitch darkness in which these people blunder, calling their ignorance 'knowledge'.

Therefore, when I noticed how the various governments on the one hand, and the different channels on the other hand, do not dare to bring to light the other side of the truth, which is deliberately kept concealed from the intellectual arena, I decided that it was my duty to write a book, in an Arabic version and another English version, that points out where the real malaise lies, a malaise that afflicts virtually every human being on earth, though with different symptoms: the wide diversity in the symptoms of the disease from region to region should not hide the fact that it is basically the same disease that afflicts all nations of the world.

There is no avoiding the fact that no nation is conquered by other nations until it has first brought down destruction on itself.

What I propose to do in this book is to revive many terms as they were introduced by the Almighty Lord; I will also try to establish connections among the terms – fighting for instance is discussed in connection with 'piety'; the pious will be defined, as well as his relation with other people, and his role in establishing God's kingdom on earth.

I also discuss how the prophets conceived the distinction between 'jihad' and fighting, in an integrated and exact system, a system that sets exactly each concept in contrast with its counterpart, develops it and sheds light on it: and the result is a whole network, well designed and constructed, without any flaw or contradiction in it.

I try in this book to focus on man and his role in Allah's kingdom on earth; I consider man as a building block that continues the march of those who have gone by. It is hoped that this book will bring people a little out of the present darkness, that it will be a way out of the present chaos in which mankind is immersed at the moment, and which engulfs and stifles human nature. We may never lose hope, as the light of Allah, the light that His books radiate has been our best guide, the best source of evidence. So let me start now in the Name of Allah, and I praise Him, now and for ever, and pray Him for support.

CHAPTER ONE

NETWORK OF *TAGHOOTS* (EVIL IDOLS) IN THE EARTH

A Historical Overview

Since the time man was in the cave until today, he either dominated or was dominated by the stick of *taghoot*, or tyranny. Everything has changed, but the stick, and its holder, have not changed: on the contrary, the stick-holder has sophisticated his tools, putting science and religion to his service; God's religion has been misinterpreted in a way that made of it an opium that stifles life.

(It is necessary at this point to interrupt our discussion for a discussion in a few line of the word *taghoot*, the Qur'anic word that plays such a major role in our search. The *taghoot* is basically a form of political tyranny, so let's look at its etymology in Arabic. The word *'taghoot'* is derived from the verb *'tagha'*; and when we say of a disbeliever that he did this, that he *'tagha'*, it denotes that his disbelief has gone beyond all limits. As a transitive verb, when we say that someone has been *'tagha'* (in the passive voice) by the devil, we mean that the devil diverted him from uprightness. When we say of a man that he *'tagha'* we mean that he was exceedingly unjust, or oppressive. A person who is known for *'tughyan'* is haughty, arrogant and extravagant; a person who trespasses the limits of uprightness and justice. If you find writers avoiding an investigation of '*taghoot*', it is because they are too scared of a tyrant to expose his ways; and yet we badly need researchers to examine such a character in depth, and to reflect on such concepts again and again.)

But how does tyranny emerge? How can a tyrant enslave another human being, a whole nation, or several nations? We have several answers to these questions.

When Saddam Hussein's government of Iraq crumbled, people watched on TV screens ghastly and crushing chaos, which involved all forms of plunder, burglary, and rape. Viewers were stunned and unbelieving, but what such horrible events teach us are two things:

First: That the poor Iraqi people were ignorant of history on the one hand, and unaware on the other hand of the plans of the White House for creating 'democratic governments'. It transpires from reviewing history that when a tyrant died or was assassinated in olden times he left behind great chaos, as the nation would be without system or law; great anarchy and terror reigned everywhere for some time after a dictator's disappearance. Such unbearable condition would be inducement enough for people to search for and later to give allegiance to a new tyrant, with the terrible and indelible memory of the interregnum reminding them of the dire alternative to the absence of a political authority.

Second: After the master of the White House announced to his army, in the hearing of the public, that the mission had been accomplished and completed, that the number of casualties was limited, and the scheduled chaos was at an end, the real chaos was ushered. Killing started, and the White House has ever since been looking for a way out of the quagmire of chaos and killing which it has itself brought about. This glaringly shows the ignorance of the White House's consultants, American and Arab alike, of the part played by the Islamic religion in this part of the world. What the world is witnessing today is only one page of a whole book of wonders and lessens which has not been studied; a book which will not come to an end by the mere withdrawing of the American army from Iraq.

For my part, I seek enlightenment in the Qur'an, where I read the following words of the Almighty Allah:

"Come to common terms as between us and you: that we worship none but Allah; that we associate no partners with Him; that we do not erect, from among ourselves, lords and patrons other than Allah." (3: 64)

We can note that the present hierarchy emanates from the absence of equality and equity, from misrepresentation of the fundamentals of Islam, and from taking associates to Allah in control, rule, and legislation; whereas Allah created man to apply His immutable law. About that we may get further enlightenment from the following words of the Lord's in the Qur'an:

"He said: 'Get you [man and the devil] down, both of you, – all together, from the Garden, with enmity one to another: but if, as is sure, there comes to you guidance from Me, whosoever follows My guidance, will not lose his way, nor fall into misery. But whosoever turns away from My Message, verily for him is a life narrowed down, and We shall raise him up blind on the Day of Judgment.' " (20: 123-124)

Thinking of the above verse, can you find a people anywhere who lead a life narrower than that of the Muslims today? A people who are massacred without any reason they can comprehend, a people who are unable to rule themselves, or to exploit the natural resources under their feet! Such people must be a prey to other nations which, for their part, are suffering from motives of avarice and an obsession with dominance (about that further down). But let me give more attention here to the concept of *taghoot* (the evil idol), its manifestations, its history and evolution.

The family of the evil idols consists of numerous branches: these branches are even on the increase; they all walk in the steps of Pharaoh, despite the many variations in appearance. The essence remains the same: such man is always the source of dread and hatred, mingled with devotion and admiration; he is in all cases surrounded and supported by a loyal group of society, which is the sap that supplies him with nourishment.

This leads us to the necessity of defining 'terrorism'. In dictionaries we find the following about 'terrorism':

"The use of force, threatening, and frightening violence, and the spilling of blood, particularly for a political reason; or using coercion, to a point of exceeding terror and dread, for the attaining of a certain target." [1]

Now if we look at the emergence of all the governments of the earth today we find that the definition of 'terrorism' applies fully to them, though such violence or terrorism as used is called with various ennobling terms, such as 'struggle' or 'revolution'; those who lead such movements are called heroes and martyrs. But after things were firmly in the hands of the evil network, it started to use the term 'terrorism' to describe similar attempts made by others; and when a hundred and seventy representatives from those countries gathered to define 'terrorism' they could not agree on a definition they could adopt, although terrorism had for some time been a common dictionary word. The reader may, if he/she so likes, refer to a standard dictionary to ascertain this

---

1   See Al-Munjed fi Llughah, Pub. Dar al-Mashreq; dist. Al-Maktabah al-Sahrqiyah; 2nd ed. 1987. See also entry in Random House Dictionary.

point. Will Durant did in fact well perceive this fact when he said in his *Story of Civilization:*

"Every state begins in compulsion; but the habits of obedience become the content of conscience, and soon every citizen thrills with loyalty to the flag." (Vo. 1, P. 24. Pub. Simon & Schuster, 1963)

Nations of the world have long struggled against the *taghoot*; and the *taghoot* has himself struggled to disguise his color, name and slogans: he has continually improved on the form of his tyranny, and has worn mask after mask. He may say, "In God we trust," although he separates religion from state, allotting religion, in its disfigured condition, to God, while he secures the state to himself. Or he may raise such terms as human rights, justice, homeland, nationality, security requirements, and the list is long; while he lets other parts of the world go on just as they are; he lets things even deteriorate in certain regions. Now there is conflict between the evil idol of the east and that of the west, when the western idol regards his eastern counterpart as backward, ossified and inhuman; and he has succeeded in taking in some simple people, who now chant the praise of the *taghoot* in his new disguise. Man is now at a loss, which of the two evils, the western or the eastern, is lesser.

Let us recall the bell attached to the neck of a ram, so that the other sheep in the flock follow the sound of the bell and keep together, following whatever direction is chosen for them, and with the dog guarding and monitoring. Now the evil *taghoots* of the earth have discovered bells that they attach to the neck of some individuals, and they employ the army to serve as their dog which keeps jumping around the flock – not to protect it, but to perpetuate the *taghoot's* (the evil idol) settling on God's throne. You may just pass by the building of *taghoots*, the United Nations, in New York City, and observe on many metal posts pieces of cloth in different colors, designated as 'flags', for which poets and artists chant. You can observe how the *taghoots*, whether politicians or clergymen, wave those pieces of cloth to drive the masses to frenzy, to arouse in them the love of the homeland and the sentiments of patriotism, something that had been inculcated in their minds since their tender years, and firmly established by impassioned songs and poetry.

When the *taghoot* says, in the course of his speech, 'May God bless this country,' you find the public excited and elated. Indeed, Jesus, peace be on him, was aware of this game which is played by the clergy on the one hand, and by the *taghoots* of the earth on the other. He was keen on getting man out of the mantle of national allegiance to begin with, and then to get him out of the false religion. That may be noted in the following words of his:

"13: Enter ye in at the strait gate: for wide is the gate, and broad is the way, that leadeth to destruction, and many there be which go in thereat:

14: Because strait is the gate, and narrow is the way, which leadeth unto life, and few there be that find it.

15: Beware of false prophets, which come to you in sheep's clothing, but inwardly they are ravening wolves.

16: Ye shall know them by their fruits. Do men gather grapes of thorns, or figs of thistles?

17: Even so every good tree bringeth forth good fruit; but a corrupt tree bringeth forth evil fruit.

18: A good tree cannot bring forth evil fruit, neither can a corrupt tree bring forth good fruit.

19: Every tree that bringeth not forth good fruit is hewn down, and cast into the fire.

20: Wherefore by their fruits ye shall know them."
(Matthew, 7: 13-20)

Elsewhere in the same book he says:

28: Come unto me, all ye that labour and are heavy laden, and I will give you rest.

29: Take my yoke upon you, and learn of me; for I am meek and lowly in heart: and ye shall find rest unto your souls.

30: For my yoke is easy, and my burden is light.

(Matthew, 11: 28-30)

On the following pages I go through some historical varieties of tyranny, then I discuss how the kingdom of Allah may be erected on the earth; I list the characteristics of Allah's kingdom, and discuss whether the *taghoot* has a part in such a kingdom, in view of the principle that a kingdom that is established by force alone is doomed to a speedy collapse.

Historically, the *taghoot* has appeared in many forms, some of the most salient being the following:

1. Tyranny,   2. Dictatorship,   3. Totalitarianism,

4. Absolute rule,   5. Autocracy,   6. 'The just imam',

7. Despotism,   8. Democracy.

Let us then take these variants one by one:

1. Tyranny

Tyranny first emerged inside the family, and later it was transferred to the sphere of the whole society. In the family, you can note how the males – fathers, brothers, or husbands – oppress the females. In the state, you see how monarchs oppress their nations, hiding behind such mottos as: "God, monarch, homeland!"; and the monarch poses as a patriarch who protects the family. And simple individuals just accept this situation; the monarch reigns, assuming that he is inherently entitled to the position of monarchy, that man himself belongs to him. Therefore, a monarch gives himself the prerogative of issuing edicts to his 'people', putting them right when he thinks they have deviated from the desired direction – according to him, it is he alone who knows what is best for 'my people', while the masses are immature, or they know nothing, so it is not right for them to object.

In the tyrannical system, a whole people surrender their will to a monarch, who is a tyrant. It was the Byzantines who introduced the term 'tyranny' in politics, and at the beginning it was an honorific title that the emperor conferred on whoever he chose. The term is more common in the West than in the East, and the former especially uses this word to legitimize its colonization of other lands.

The Western master used to apply the term 'tyrants' to Ottoman rulers, while both in fact were equally evil, since they both subjugated man to their service. It was with this conception about the Ottomans that the Western tyrant used his superior sophistication to study the Ottoman rule, and then destroyed it; an example of such studies is that of Bernet, the French physician[2], of Turkey, India, Iran, and some other regions. The point is that the tyrant sought pretexts for his tyranny, as we may notice in the distribution of the legacy of Louis XIV. New forms of tyranny have been introduced all the time, as may be witnessed in the democratic and legislative tyranny (the majority tyranny). And when a new phase of tyranny was ushered in to replace an older one, it was ennobled with such designations as 'new steps towards enlightenment and freedom', the latest of such term being 'reformation'.

---

2   *The Production Pattern (Asian)*, by Anderson, p. 397

2. Dictatorship:

Used first by the Romans, a dictator was a person granted exceptional authority – having the armed forces, the state and the public under his dominance. The Romans specified a limited term for a dictator, but he used to sidetrack such term, prolonging the dictatorship, citing the pretext of emergency, the necessity of imposing order, or the wish of the public, the need for forcing law and order, protecting the state's security, or defending the interests of the country.

It is worth our while to specify the distinction between the modern and ancient concepts of dictatorship. In the past, dictatorship was understood to be associated with a special period, i.e. after a certain disaster; but in modern times, a dictator is there to stay indefinitely; he sees himself as meriting that position inherently, that he is right to cling to the throne, even after the end of the historical crisis – we have ample evidence of this in the Arab World. You see how an Arab dictator hides behind Israel for a continuation of his rule, claiming that there is national, religious or regional need for his existence. In spite of the fact that the Arabs have recognized Israel and signed peace with it, the state of emergency is still imposed, and the dictator is still sitting on both people's necks and minds.

3. Totalitarianism:

Another mask that is used by the evil idol is collective tyranny, in which a leader employs terror, violence and subjugation to hold in his hand all authority; and he makes sure that the whole nation surrender blindly to his commands. The state is here the ultimate fact – it is the source of interpreting or organizing anything. You can find in history any number of totalitarian rulers, two of whom are Hitler and Mussolini. When a leader gives his opinion, it is the 'people's' opinion; usually such a leader would inflame people's feelings with fiery speeches, coaxing, bribing, intimidation, and the leader's claim that he speaks for the whole nation, representing what is fair and just.

4. Absolute Rule:

We have here a government that takes it its right to rule without any limitation to its authority; there is no surveillance over it: all under the pretext of political and social order. That did take place in some European countries, where a government demanded unlimited authority, that it should be absolutely free in exercising its power, that its dominance was to be supreme and total; and that included that a ruler might not be deposed under any circumstances. It was supposed then that a king was appointed by God's will, that he was seated on the throne by authorization from God, and in this way the public were duped, since they had no knowledge of Allah or of Allah's laws.

5. Autocracy:

Autocracy may be defined as an arbitrary and one-man's rule, an individual who can abolish the constitution at will. Such government may be met with in different varieties, all characterized with tyranny and oppression. An individual hides here behind an elastic constitution, and laws that he can manipulate as his caprice leads him.

6. The Just Imam (or: the Inspired Tyrant)

This is a yet another branch of this evil tree. Those who advocate such rule believe that an inspired tyrant is the right person to preserve the ummah's (Muslim nation's) unity, that he would refine the moral system and disseminate knowledge, and that he has possession of the magic key to erecting this illusive nation.

And yet, the dilemma of nations is not in spotting a just imam, but in finding the just system. We may conclude as much from a Qur'anic verse:

"and follow the way of those who turn to Me (in love)" (30, 15), where the Lord does not say, 'follow those who turn to Me;" it is rather a system (a way) that one is to follow, and that people have long missed. As long as the system is there, there can be appointed an individual who can shoulder the task. Thinking of the 'inspired imam', we may regard the example of a child mounted on a donkey and leading a large troop of camels.

It may be noted that the term 'inspired tyrant' or 'just dictator' is self-contradictory: how can tyranny and justice come together? It is rather like having contaminated water and pure water in one glass: such water is not pure no matter how someone insists on calling it pure.

7. The Despot

It was Archilochus, a Greek poet of the seventh century B.C.[3] who was the first to use the term 'despotism' or 'despot'. A despot is an irresponsible person, who brings destruction both on himself, through injustice and sin, and on others, through exceeding all bounds in diverting them from the right way; he is indeed a reckless man who can do good neither to himself nor to others. What he practices is yet another form of tyranny in his rule. In the West, it was considered a duty to kill a despot; some laws were even set for killing him. And yet this word did not sound detestable until the West did actually experience the rule of despots.

In such rule, the constitution refers to the whims of the despot; everything is based on absolute yielding to his authority: the executive, legislative, and judicial authorities are firmly in his hands and in his name. Socrates and Plato considered this kind of rule to be the worst on earth, as it comes about through usurpation and assassination. If you look into the titles conferred on the despot you find him addressed as 'your majesty,' 'the benefactor,'

3   Abdul Fattah Imam, *The Despot*, Alam Al-Ma'rifah.

11

'the great,' and 'the life-long ruler'; it is not uncommon to find such an individual having megalomania.

8. Democracy:

Some people would conclude that all evil emanates from running after authority, and from such vices as greed and rapacity; and the alternative for some is that many parties should be formulated although, as we see in reality, party-men self-seekers try to secure for themselves the utmost of public interests under such slogans as 'public service'; making a show in the meanwhile of serving the public, and not forgetting to make use of the most high-sounding rhetoric, with which they hypnotize their hearers. They would not hesitate to make promises that they never mean to fulfill, promises to realize equality among people, and 'democracy' would be their catchword. In short, such fraudulent politicians would not hesitate to put to use any and each means that may bring them closer to the seat of power (sitting on the necks of the people they claim to serve). People will certainly endure such disastrous rule as long as they do not heed the words of Allah when He teaches us that calamities are "from yourselves," (3:165) and are "by permission of Allah," (3: 166).

It is as a certain poet has put it: "Why should you blame the wolf when he attacks, if the shepherd is an enemy of the flock!" This is very true, for if I am my own enemy out of my ignorance, why should I blame the wolves of the earth?

*   *   *

It transpires from our survey so far that though man seems to feel indignant at times and break free from one ring of tyranny and despotism, he would introduce some changes, usurp people's right and redistributes positions. The latest variety in this connection is democracy: here we find the *taghoot* disguising himself in the skin of the lamb, and choosing this designation which is calculated to put people's minds at rest; it is palatable enough to believe in the illusion of people's ruling themselves. What actually happens is that people have only broken free from one form of tyranny to fall into another; and they have no idea where their salvation lies. In the democratic trap, people are deluded into thinking that there is a supreme authority which has no other authority above it, without someone having control of it, that such authority has equal dominance over all. People are taken in by the phrase of free elections, while behind such elections there are concealed all kinds of parties, so-called national, religious, or democratic, while they are headed by ringleaders who are hired by one of the *taghoots* of the earth, a member of the evil network which has dominance in the earth, although bickering erupts inside it from time to time.

Let's read the words of the Almighty Lord in the Qur'an about the *taghoots* and their followers:

"Here is an army rushing blindly with you (into fire). Those who are already in the fire say: 'No word of welcome for them. Lo! They will roast at the Fire.' They say: 'Nay, but you misleaders, for you there is no word of welcome. Ye prepared this for us by your misleading. Now hapless is the plight.' They say: 'Our Lord! Whoever did prepare this for us, oh, give him double portion of the Fire!' And they say: 'What aileth us that we behold not men whom we were wont to count among the wicked? Did we take them wrongly for a laughing-stock, or have our eyes missed them?' Lo! That is very truth: the wrangling of the dwellers in the Fire. Say unto them, O Muhammad: 'I am only a warner, and there is no God but Allah, the One, the Absolute, Lord of the heavens and the earth and all that is between them, the Mighty, the Pardoning.' Say: 'It is tremendous tidings, whence ye turn away.' " (38: 59-68)

And to conclude:

It is right what some have said that the tyrants are human monsters that have appeared throughout history, dominating nations with iron and fire. It is a truth that Allah reveals to us that both the tyrants and the people they dominate are 'like the cattle, nay but they are farther astray,' (the Qur'an, 25: 44); and in the same spirit, the Bible describes the children of Israel at as certain stage of their history as worse than beasts. It is told us by God in His scriptures that to force people to do something, under the pretext of doing it for the good of man is tyranny: Allah has raised man and given him precedence over all creation, and given him free will, as we notice in the following verse from the Qur'an:

"Say: 'the truth is from your Lord': let him who will, believe, and let him who will, reject it." (18: 29)

I hope our discussion so far makes it clear that a pharaoh is a pharaoh, though he will come in endless forms and roles, and no matter how different he might appear to us in looks, behavior and designations.

My intention in the above historical survey has been to prepare the ground for the 'deified' *taghoot*, what prepares the way for him to come, and what helps in making it impossible for him to survive in the earth.

CHAPTER TWO

TRANSGRESSION IN THE QURAN

Transgression [*tughyan* which is, in Arabic, derived from the same root as *taghoot*] has been described to us by God in the various scriptures; and we find in the Qur'an that the existence of *tughyan* in the earth is inevitable: "Nay, but man transgresses all bounds." (96: 6)

According to the Qur'an, it is the responsibility of man himself that transgression should happen; it emanates from his own character:

"His companion will say: "Our Lord! I did not make him transgress, but he was himself far astray." (50: 27)

It is crystal clear in the words of the Almighty that a *taghoot* (an evil idol) is himself accountable for his conduct, that his conduct is by his own volition. As for how to get rid of such transgressor, the Qur'an also describes the right technique for that, and the conditions that must be realized before a *taghoot* should disappear. These techniques or conditions are no more than two: By avoiding a *taghoot* he will vanish, and by disbelieving in him he will vanish. When the Qur'an declares: "Serve Allah, and eschew the *taghoot*," (16: 36) it means that you do not fight against the tyrant, nor do you kill him; you do not, on the other hand, work in his service. To disbelieve in the *taghoot* means that not the slightest trace of love should dwell in one's heart for the *taghoot* or his supporters, even if the latter are one's parents, children, brothers or spouses. That much may be learnt from the above verse about eschewing the *taghoot*, and from other verses, such as,

"Those who eschew the evil idol, – and do not fall into its worship, – and turn to Allah, searching for what He commands, and adhering to it, – for them is good news: so announce the good news to My servants, – Those who listen to the word, and follow the best meaning in it: those who are the ones whom Allah has guided, and those who are the ones endued with understanding." (39, 17-18)

To accomplish the discarding of *taghoot*, there are certain requisites to be fulfilled in this life, for the Almighty alerts us in the above verses that before the *taghoot* vanishes (the good news in the above verses), believers must realize certain qualities, namely accepting Allah's guidance, and being endued with understanding; they should, as we shall see, hold to the 'firm hand-hold'. This is a basic aspect of the elite who are bent on erecting the kingdom of Allah on the earth. It must be evident, therefore, why we are called upon to fulfill the requirements of such group in the Qur'an, without neglecting any verse of it.

It will be noted in the list of verses below how the Almighty Lord connects supporting the *taghoot* to disbelief, while He pairs the concept of belief to the shunning of *taghoot*, so that the former two pairs of traits seem synonymous, and the two latter ones seem synonymous. Let's look at the Qur'an:

"Of those who reject faith the patrons are the evil ones;" (2: 257)
"Allah is the Protector of the righteous." (45: 19)
"Serve Allah, and eschew the evil one;" (16: 36)

"Whoever rejects the *taghoot* and believes in Allah has grasped the most trustworthy hand-hold, that never breaks." (2: 256)
"and those who reject faith fight in the cause of the *taghoot*," (4: 76)
"Those who believe fight in the cause of Allah;" (4: 76)

This support, whether of the *taghoot* or of the Almighty God is, as Allah makes it clear, connected at the same time to the development of the earth: that is so because man's siding with the *taghoot* is conducive to man's moving from light to darkness, from a constructive attitude to a destructive one, and from faith to disbelief. On the other hand, man's allying with Allah will lead to an observable result: man will move from darkness to light, from idleness to constructiveness, to safety and settling. We may learn this from the following verses of the Qur'an:

"Of those who reject faith the patrons are the evil ones: from light they will lead them forth into the depths of darkness." (2:257)
"Allah is the Protector of those who have faith: from the depths of darkness He will lead them forth into light." (2:257)

Allah contrasts good thinking and faith with false talk: "but shun the abomination of idols, and shun the word that is false." (22:30);
"and He hath set uncleanness upon those who have no sense." (10:100);
"Thus Allah layeth ignominy upon those who believe not." (6:125)

It will be noted that this link between the shunning of uncleanness and the shunning of *taghoot* in Allah's law has been misrepresented by the clerics, so that you find them in only one of two states:

- Either sitting in the lap of the *taghoot* and ignominy; or
- Combating *taghoot* to replace him and be the new *taghoot*.

This has only been possible after the meaning of jihad was misconceived, as was the meaning of Islam itself; and the latter is no longer perceived but as embodied in an organization, although such organization is itself forbidden in religion. Indeed, Jesus was quite mindful of this degradation when he warned:

"beware of the leaven of the Pharisees and of the Sadducees." (Matthew, 16: 6)

And when his followers failed to understand this, he explained: "How is it that ye do not understand that I spake it not to you concerning bread, and that ye should beware of the leaven of the Pharisees and of the Sadducees?" (Matthew, 16: 11)

You may wonder if there were other people before us who submitted to the *taghoot*, and what was the retribution? Browsing through the Qur'an one would find so many examples, as we may read in the following examples about Noah's people, Thamud and 'Ad [two peoples often described in the Holy Qur'an]:

"And before them, the people of Noah, for that they were most unjust and most insolent transgressors." (53: 52)

"The Thamud and the 'Ad, people branded as false, the stunning calamity (was sent on them.) But the Thamud, – they were destroyed by a terrible storm of thunder and lightning." (69: 4-5)

Don't you see, O men, that what brings disasters on you is the united power of the tyrants of the earth!

Let's refer again to the Qur'an:

"It is the revelation that comes to you from your Lord that increases in most of them their obstinate rebellion and blasphemy." (5: 68)

"Have you not seen those unto whom a portion of the scripture has been given how they believe in idols and false deities." (4: 51)

We may notice how tyranny will for ever take on new disguises, now going under the apparel of a missionary, now the appearance of a democrat, and now as the three authorities. But we have been solemnly commanded to shun him, by not working for him, and by equally not combating him. By failing to do either measure a grave fate will be waiting for us: it is indeed a condition that we are living at the moment! That is fair retribution, since most nations appeal to the *taghoot* rather than to Allah, and so they live in darkness, and such rays of light as may exist do not serve to shed enough light for nations to go ahead. It must be evident then that the reviving of the concept of eschewing the *taghoot* is a vital requirement in our age, since there are everywhere tyrants who usurp the position of God, and nations which concede to them, and submit to their command and work for them. We may say about them what the Almighty says in the Qur'an:

"Allah will throw back their mockery on them, and give them rope in their trespasses; so they will wander like blind ones to and fro." (2: 15)

And says elsewhere: "We shall leave them in their trespasses, to wander in distraction." (6: 110)

What happens at present is that history throws us from one tyrant to another, as long as we do not recognize the technique of resisting of the *taghoot* (the evil idol) – though it is a very simple technique, consisting in:

"Eschew the *taghoot*"

And that is to say:

Do not work for him;

And:

Do not fight him;

And:

Turn your back to him, and submit to Allah in obedience. That is to say, the enemy is not the *taghoot*, but members of your family who work for him. It is such people that Jesus had in mind when he said: "And man's foes shall be they of his own household." (Matthew, 10: 36)

Not different from what we recite in the Qur'an:
"Truly, among your wives and your children are some that are enemies to yourselves: so beware of them!" (64: 14)

Therefore, if the *taghoot* decides to eliminate someone, he will not come himself to slay him, but will send some members of that person's family who work for him; they function as the dog who skips about the flock, and the *taghoot* can attain his desire because it is as an Arab poet has said:

Why should you blame the wolf,
If the shepherd himself is an enemy of his sheep!

CHAPTER THREE

Injustice and Ignorance

The Kingdom of Allah that Prophet Muhammad, peace be upon him, established had hardly started its course when its structure started to crack – that is when the Muslims split into Sunni and Shiite and then fell on each other in ongoing conflict. Until this day, both camps are wallowing in a quagmire of ignorance, while the path of good guidance stares them in the face, in the words of Adam's better son (as reported in the Qur'an, 5: 28) when he told his killing-intent brother: " 'even if thou stretch out thy hand against me to kill me, I shall not stretch out my hand against thee to kill thee, lo! I fear Allah, the Lord of the Worlds."

And now, it is fourteen centuries since the advent of Islam, but man is still unjust and ignorant, and the Muslims are still involved in killing and ignorance: hence the *ummah's* (the Muslim nation's) wallowing in an abyss of stagnation and corruption. Evidence for this claim can be met with anywhere in the so-called 'Muslim World', a gross misnomer, when the Muslims are sharply divided into Sunni and Shiite, Arabs and Turks, Kurds and Afghanis, and so forth. A unifying Islam seems no more than a nostalgic mirage.

When men succumb to their own injustice and ignorance of the teachings of religion, they will inevitably come under the dominance of the earth's *taghoots* (the evil idols), who have assumed their position either through inheritance, the use of force, or the new smart dominance, democracy. That the *taghoots* have acquired permanence on earth has led to several phenomena, the salient of which being:

First: The absence of a constant and just law that is unanimously accepted by mankind (the global village); under such law each man's duties and responsibilities will be determined, as well as his rights.

Secondly: The absence of an unbiased rule in 'the global village', which may deal in justice and fairness among people, not yielding to their biases, a rule which guarantees man's freedom and rights.

Thirdly: The absence of an authority that enjoys the power and know-how necessary for enforcing that justice, firmly, fairly and thoroughly.

Fourthly: The absence of a basis of knowledge and an established method for launching that fair rule. That for one thing; for another, the absence of a clear knowledge of the way to developing such an authority that is capable of enforcing the wished-for justice.

It is no wonder, in view of the above drawbacks, that societies cry for a way out of the quagmires in which they live, often resorting to terrorism, following in the steps of the *taghoot*, rather than in the steps of the prophets. It is so since people have not yet recognized the way of the prophets. Unmindful of the fact that the world is now literally 'a global village', they feel their only hope to be in choosing the best among the *taghoots* (the evil idols) of the earth, forgetting that all *taghoots* are evil. We may seek enlightenment about that in the Qur'an, which relates to us how Pharaoh tried to convince Moses and Aaron that they had no alternative to succumbing to him, but Moses, peace be upon him, retorted, as the Qur'an reports:

"And this is the favor with which you do reproach me, – that you have enslaved the Children of Israel!" (26: 22)

It is perhaps in order here to elaborate a little further about injustice in the history of mankind and the latter's ignorance of the facts of religion: we have the example of the Jews when they rejected Christ, waiting for a Christ that was unknown and even nonexistent; in this condition they carry on, not following Noah or Abraham, peace be on them; at the same time they reject Muhammad, peace be upon him.

In the same way, those who claim to be followers of Christ, the Christians, do not actually follow him, which was indeed predicted by him when he said:

"But those mine enemies, which would not that I should reign over them, bring hither, and slay them before me." (Luke, 19: 26)

What Christ's followers actually did was to ally with his enemies who had rejected him. In this way, they are followers of neither Noah, Abraham, nor Moses, peace be upon them; at the same time they reject Muhammad, peace be upon him, without looking into the religion he taught.

As for Muhammad's followers, the Muslims, they are seeking to revive a religion that existed 1400 years ago; and they hardly know the reality about that religion. What they actually do is to oscillate between an ancient, local tyranny, under whose weight they groan; and an illusory and glamorous democracy, discarded by even its progenitors. Enough evidence we have in

Afghanistan's Taliban and the Iranian government. All parties would assert that

'Islam provides the solution',

an Islam that they do not understand. Ask any Muslim about the fundamentals of Islam and he would say, naively enough, "They are to witness that there is no god but Allah; prayer, fasting, pilgrimage and paying the ordained charity '*zakat*'." Imams would call from above their pulpits, each Friday,

"Prayer is the mainstay of religion; if one performs
it regularly he has erected religion."

And so prayer is performed five times a day, everywhere in the earth, but even so, Islam is not enforced anywhere in the earth, in the 'global village'; so how is it, you may wonder, that 'the mainstay of religion' is not solving mankind's problems?

We have enough evidence in what is taking place in front of us, but Allah sees all, and He should suffice as witness.

You may ask any Muslim, "Can you cite evidence from the Holy Qur'an to support your claim that the above are the fundamentals of Islam?" and he will be nonplussed. It only shows how deluded Muslims are, when they claim to be followers of Muhammad, peace be upon him: what they cling to is something else, and not what is in the Holy Qur'an, so that they hold in their hands what belies their claim.

The fundamentals of Islam are actually there in the Qur'an, but Muslims skim through it without comprehending it, nor do they believe in its message; one may be right to say they are not cognizant of it.

This problem of the true religion is so hard for two reasons:

One reason is this tripartite division (Christian, Muslim and Jew); and within each group there are the secular and religious-minded, the latter claiming to know well their religion; then the secular are further divided into leftist, liberal and conservative. The conservative are subdivided and know so little about their religion.

The other reason is that the religion of Islam raises five subjects that are ignored by those who claim to be devout followers of it, and these five points are bypassed in Muslims' continuous wrangling over the truth of religion.

You may ask any Muslim for instance, "You claim you to believe in the Qur'an: so, being your Scripture, what topics are discussed in it?" You may be sure that you will not find one common answer among Muslims!

So how can a Muslim expound his religion when he himself is ignorant of it, though he makes a big claim of being a dedicated follower of it?

How can one believe in something that he is ignorant of?

Muslims cling to a religion that they inherited but not comprehend, despite their assertion that 'Islam provides the solution.'

What a Muslim really embraces are principles that run counter to what is stated in the Holy Qur'an.

Let's quote in this connection the late Muhammad Mutawalli al-Sha'rawee, when he says, "If we survey our [the Muslims'] condition today we are sure to find that though we are classified as a Muslim community, we are indeed not so; we are only counted as Muslims for bearing the name of Islam."[4]

"So how can such a Muslim community be realized," he goes on to say. "It is by knowing the reality of our religion."

What we have above is an admission by the foremost conventional Muslim cleric that we do not understand the reality of our religion. And I count that as a first ray of a horizon: it is something that some Muslim spiritual leaders begin to perceive that Muslims have lost the right path. What we do not perceive is that the reason they have lost the right path, which they crave to find, is that they fail to fathom the meaning of a Qur'anic verse like:

"Nay, but their contrivance is made seeming fair for those who disbelieve and they are kept from the right road. He whom Allah sends astray, for him there is no guide." (13: 33)

Now when we start teaching children the Arabic language, we begin with a definition of speech or discourse. 'Speech' we say is:

1. An utterance[5]
2. Complex.
3. Purposeful.
4. Divided into 'name', 'verb' and 'article, preposition, etc.'
5. Expressive.
6. Declensional, subject to position as determined in grammar (a word being marked with one of the four diacritics, the 'u', 'i', 'a', and 'none'.)

---

4   In his book, *This Is Islam*, pub. Dar al-Kutub al-Misriyah, p. 43.

5   As in the authoritative book '*Ajroomiyah*', by Abu Abdullah Muhammad, s/o Muhammad, s/o Dawood al-Sihajee, published by Mustafa al-Babee al-Halabee bookstore, Cairo

And we go on to give more details about when a word should have the diacritic 'u', when it is a noun in a certain position, or a present tense if no 'subjunctive article' precedes it: and on and on go the rules of correct grammar. But as the child struggles and toils to learn those rules he knows nothing about the content of words. Then we start once more to teach him what an utterance is, and we go back to the letters of the alphabet he had learnt from his mother, teaching him how to shape them on paper; we make him inscribe those letters again and again. Later we teach a child how to put those letters together, making him aware that any change in formation will have a corresponding change in function. We teach him the parts of speech, how words bear meaning, then we teach him how to differentiate noun from verb from preposition, conjunction, article, etc., and last we introduce him to inflection and declension.

More than fifteen years of a child's life are spent in this long process, more than fifteen long years in which all efforts on the part of the mother and school collaborate. And by the end of his secondary course he will not have had command of his own language; and let's remember that language is just one subject that deals with one topic, speech. But when we think of religion we find that five overlapping topics are involved in it; the five topics being:

- Allah
- Man
- Allah's Scriptures
- Allah's creation
- Allah's laws

As a child loses sight of the essence of language in his effort to untangle the forming bricks of language, we may say here that man will not get at the system ordained by the Almighty as long as we make him spend his life spelling out the smallest details of religion. So let us go at once to the fundamentals of Islam, which are, in contrast with what is inculcated by the clerics, to be found in the following verse from the Lord's words in the Holy Qur'an:

"Say: My Lord forbids only indecencies, such of them as are apparent and such as are within, and sin and wrongful oppression, and that you associate with Allah that for which no warrant has been revealed , and that you tell concerning Allah that which you know not." (7: 33)

There is an evident difference between the fundamentals of Islam as established by the above verse, and what imams teach everywhere!

As by the Qur'an, the fundamentals of Islam are:

1. Forbidding indecencies, such of them as are apparent and such as are within,
2. Forbidding sin
3. Forbidding wrongful oppression
4. Forbidding associating with Allah that for which no warrant has been revealed, and
5. Forbidding that you tell concerning Allah that which you know not.

So the above are the fundamentals of Islam, and not what the ruler-controlled clerics teach. And again one wonders, what is the right doctrine? Where do we start?

Indeed, what God's prophets and messengers taught is essentially the same religion, as we learn from the following verse from the Qur'an:

"The same religion He has established for you as that which He enjoined on Noah – the which We have sent by inspiration to you – and that which We enjoined on Abraham, Moses, and Jesus: namely, that you should remain steadfast in religion, and make no divisions therein: to those who worship other things than Allah, hard is the way to which you call them. Allah chooses to Himself those whom He pleases, and guides to Himself those who turn to Him." (42: 13)

So as we see, religion is erected on two principles
1. That you should remain steadfast in religion, and
2. That you make no divisions therein.

How well this parallels what Jesus, peace be upon him, taught, as reported in the Bible:
"Think not that I am come to destroy the law, or the prophets: I am not come to destroy, but to fulfil." (Matthew, 5: 17)

In contrast, see how those who claim to follow the prophets and messengers of Allah are not steadfast in religion at all, as the above verse ordains, while they do make divisions within religion.
They are divided into so many factions: Sunni, Shiite, Shafiite, Hanbalites, sufi, and so on and so forth. And yet they assert that they are following in the steps of Allah's prophets.

If we reflect carefully on God's messengers, we find in the Qur'an that their way was the same; let's read:

"The path of those whom You have favored." (1: 7)

God's religion is vividly described in the Qur'an: it is the way to which all the prophets adhered; and Allah commands us to follow in the steps of His prophets to erect His religion. Hence we may say that the human element, the building block, is one of the main elements for a realization of religion and the establishing of society. And in view of the above we can set some rules:

1. That the first and basic element in building a society is the raising of the individual 'the building block' in the Muslim society, the **submitting** element (i.e. responding to Allah), the so-far nonexistent building block, who should be striving for the establishment of religion in the earth, and who denounces any partisan divisions into sects, parties, races or nations. That is how one understands the prophets' admonition, as reported in the Qur'an, 'Is there not among you any right-minded man?' (11: 78)

2. That harmony and accord should characterize their relationships; and that is related to identifying a unifying target for which this building block or nucleus devotes his life.

3. The developing of a well-constructed family, and that entails all that contributes to the unity of the family.

4. At this stage there can come into existence that nucleus, 'the submitting man', who fulfils the target for which he was placed on this planet.

5. The establishment of the Kingdom of Allah, or, as the Qur'an puts it, "Establish religion, and be not divided therein." (42: 13); that comes about through a recognition of the way of Allah and the way of *taghoot* (the evil idol).

6. That man, the nucleus, should perceive that Allah, Creator of man, has given him the freedom to choose one of two ways, the way of Allah or the way of *taghoot*.

7. That the nucleus, the building individual, perceives that when Allah created man He commanded him to break free from those who choose to follow the *taghoot*; we may refer to Christ's saying about those who choose the way of *taghoot*: " Give not that which is holy unto the

dogs, neither cast ye your pearls before swine, lest they trample them under their feet, and turn again and rend you." (Matthew, 7: 6). We have also in the Qur'an God's saying: "So proclaim that which thou art commanded, and withdraw from the idolaters." (15: 94)

8. That the nucleus has a clear view of the value of gaining this world and the value of gaining the Hereafter. Hence the words of Christ: "But seek ye first the kingdom of God, and his righteousness; and all these things shall be added unto you." (Matthew, 6: 33).

9. That the nucleus appreciates the value of prostrating himself before God.

10. That the nucleus distinguishes optional from involuntary prostration (surrender) to Allah the Almighty. The Almighty has placed man on this earth so that he may develop it, as the following verse of the Qur'an indicates: "He brought you forth to the earth and has made you husband it. So ask forgiveness of Him and turn unto Him repentant." (11: 61)

This appointment of man as a vicegerent of God in the earth is a great honoring of him, since what man does in the earth must reflect the attributes of Allah: Allah is just, and He loves to see the fruit of His justice in the earth; He loves to see the establishment of a peaceful society where there is no bloodshed, where human rights are honored – the rights of man's dignity, freedom, and ownership in the earth. In this way will man transcend the expectation of angels on the day of man's creation: the individual should be the nucleus whose duty it is to bring that about. God has specified the conditions and law of that; He has specified also the conditions for the nucleus who will be doing the building and bearing the responsibility.

Man is the only creature who produces history, science, and art. This knowledge was endowed by God, as we read in the Qur'an:

"Taught man that which he did not know." (96: 5) This means that man is the only creature capable of completing and developing God's Kingdom which was begun by the prophets. Man is also the only creature capable of evolving socially and culture: starting his life in the cave, he ascended to build astronomical observatories and to invade space; he walked on the moon, a feat which was thought impossible not long ago. Indeed, all his achievements in technology are amazing breakthroughs, and that is a fulfillment of God's promise in the Qur'an: "And [He] has made of service unto you whatsoever is in the heavens and whatsoever is in the earth," (45: 13) – but man, who has accomplished the impossible in one direction, and has proved himself capable of constructive achievement, has himself destroyed what has been built over the generations. So many statements abound that describe, in sociological or anthropological terms, the story of man, his ascent and evolution, how he created society and state. The books of history are full of such details, but we should be curious to know what Allah says about man, the nucleus, the builder of Allah's kingdom: what conditions are prescribed for this nucleus to be able to accomplish that task and to bring to completion the laying of the bricks of that structure.

Allah has sent His messengers to guide man along the way that he should follow, to develop his abilities and his tools. They taught mankind about the basics of what, according to the will of the Almighty God, is permitted and what is forbidden. This should be like a compass that shows us the right direction. When concepts and principles get confused, the foundations of the structure will be loose and it will collapse on the heads of its dwellers.

It may be agreed upon by most people that the basic foundation in establishing that Kingdom is pointing out what is permitted and what is forbidden; but where disagreement may arise is in the specification of the permitted and the forbidden; for some will include or exclude items in both sectors in view of the dictates of the temporal requirements, their personal interests, or depending on the breadth of one's vision. What we find in the words of the Lord, however, is that He succinctly defines what is allowed and what is forbidden under five heads:

1. He forbids (as we may learn for instance from the Qur'an, 7: 33) indecencies, such of them as are apparent and such as secret; He ordains prayer, so that it forbids all shameful deeds.
2. He forbids sin,
3. He forbids wrongful oppression,
4. He forbids that we associate with Allah that for which no warrant has been revealed,
5. He forbids that we tell concerning Allah that which we know not.

The above five items, combined, are all forbidden to man by Allah; His Kingdom may not have any of the above in its bases. I shall elaborate in the following chapters about the above articles, since tyranny will set in as soon as any of the five prohibited things is violated, and tyranny will, in its turn, bring mischief to society.

Whenever you see people's rights transgressed, you may be sure that one or more of the enormous sins mentioned above have been committed. This is what the following Qur'anic verse indicates:

"Whatever beings there are in the heavens and the earth do prostrate themselves to Allah (acknowledging subjection) – with good-will or in spite of themselves; so do their shadows in the mornings and evenings." (13: 15)

The same was expressed by Christ, peace be upon him, when he said: "You will know them by their fruits." (Matthew, 7: 16)

CHAPTER FOUR

System of Developing the Nucleus

A nucleus begins to develop once he realizes that mankind has just one Lord, to whom man belongs, the One God and King; that this King is the Real King; that all the others who are called kings by people are false kings, when contrasted with the True King, Allah; that this King, the True Lord, has created the heavens and the earth, has made darkness and light; that He is all pity and mercy for people; that this Kind and Merciful King, the Compassionate, created man, and taught him effective utterance; that he made a covenant with Adam and his progeny, as expressed in the Qur'an: "Choose no guardian beside Me." (17: 2)

The disbelievers, however, ascribe rivals unto their Lord; they seem to forget that the present false king (the *taghoot*), who reigns in the earth today has created nothing: of this we are reminded by the words of the True King in the Qur'an:

"O men! Here is a parable set forth! Listen to it! Those on whom, besides Allah, you call, cannot create even a fly, if they all met together for the purpose! And if the fly should snatch away anything from them, they would have no power to release it from the fly. Feeble are those who petition and those whom they petition. No just estimate have they made of Allah: for

Allah is He Who is strong and able to carry out His Will." (22: 73-74)

This Lord, the True King, the Strong and Able, for whom prostrate in submission all that is in heavens and all that is in the earth, with good-will or in spite of themselves; He Who raised the heavens without any pillars that you can see; is firmly established on the throne of authority; He Who has subjected the sun and the moon to His law, each one runs its course for a term appointed; He Who regulates all affairs, explaining the signs in detail, that you may believe with certainty in the meeting with your Lord. And it is He Who spread out the earth, and set thereon mountains standing firm, and flowing rivers; and fruit of every kind He made in pairs. He draws the night as a veil over the day. He is the Lord Who will not be pleased to see man take an associate beside Him.

This then is the first step in educating the nucleus about the Lord. And next, a nucleus needs to realize the existence of a True King and a false king (the *taghoot*): Allah, the True King, will guide the nucleus to the proper way of dealing with the actual world – that will take place after the nucleus has determined to whom he owes allegiance, to the True King or to the false king, the *taghoot*.

This free choice, giving man the right to choose, is an honoring of man, but the *taghoot* lies when he claims that it is he who has granted men freedom – that is absolutely false, as the *taghoot* never grants freedom: he actually robs people of their freedom. We have evidence enough in history, and the actual state of affairs proves that, but we call on Allah to be the best of witnesses. A *taghoot* should not fool us when he says that he does not rob people of their freedom.

Next, the nucleus is warned that we gain nothing through money, as we recite in the Qur'an:

"Not if you had spent all that is in the earth, could you have produced that affection (in the heart of believers), but Allah has done it: for He is Exalted in might, Wise." (8: 63)

As for the limits to the nucleus' responsibility, we read the following words in the Qur'an:

"You are held responsible only for yourself." (4: 84)

The idea here is that what brings a nucleus to adhere to righteousness is not sermons, nor punishments: it is rather the silent power of the model.

If this is realized by the nucleus, he will learn the immutable and constant laws of the True King. He will perceive that the *taghoot* is only there by Allah's will, and that he will also cease to be by Allah's will, since Allah is the True God, the True King. It will also be clear to the nucleus that the survival or disappearance of the *taghoot* will happen according to laws set by Allah, and that that false king, the *taghoot*, will survive as long as there is allegiance for him in the minds of people. All this may be noted in the following verse from the Qur'an:

"Verily never will Allah change the condition of a people until they change that which is in their hearts, but when Allah wills a people's punishment, there can be no turning it back, nor will they find, besides him, any to protect." (13: 11)

The idea here is that you will not be able to fill a glass with water unless the air in it is dismissed. This must be vividly perceived by the nucleus; and he must also realize that he is not taxed with the responsibility of anyone but himself; he should be cognizant of Allah's command to His messengers and prophets that people must serve Allah and eschew the *taghoot*; he must also be aware that Allah ordained to Muhammad the religion that He had ordained to Noah, to Abraham, to Moses and to Jesus, peace be on them all, and the essence of which is, as Allah has said in the Qur'an,

"Establish religion, and be not divided therein." (42: 13)

In the Qur'anic text, the starting point is in pointing out the two ways offered the human, the two ways from which to choose, that of sin, and that of virtue; that he may choose either to show gratitude to the Source of all bounty, or to disbelieve and be blind to the truth. It must be fully evident to each soul that it will be held in pledge for its deeds; then it will be a living, vigilant and self-reproaching spirit; diligent in doing what is ordained, and shunning what is prohibited. Such spirit will give painful pricks to the individual, being watchful in urging him to ascend to the safety zone. This effort to keep true to the path has been well expressed by a certain poet who said,

"I find a call inside me to what is disastrous for me
And all kinds of sores and ailment are stirred;
So how can I defeat my foe,
When he dwells within my ribs."

A spirit will have its nourishment in the words of the Almighty Allah – remember in this regard the words of Jesus, peace be upon him, quoting Moses, as reported in the Bible, "But he answered and said, It is written, Man shall not live by bread alone, but by every word that proceedeth out of the mouth of God." (Matthew, 4: 4); or refer to the Qur'an when it says, "in the remembrance of Allah do hearts find satisfaction." (13: 28) Or the other verse of the Qur'an,

"Can he who was dead, to whom We gave life, and a light whereby he can walk amongst men, be like him who is in the depths of darkness, from which he can never come out?" (6: 122)

When a spirit is alive it calls itself to account before it is called to reckoning on the Day of Judgment, and weighs its deeds before they are weighed. Thus is this spirit maintaining a delicate balance, fearing the Day of Judgment, but full of hope in its Lord's mercy. A spirit of this caliber is given insight into the significance of the signs around it: since it is not encumbered with the burden of whims, it can perceive truth for what it is, can perceive sin on one side, and virtue on the other, vividly and categorically. A spirit like this keeps watch over the individual, and gives him hard time for his shortcomings.

And step one in the training of the nucleus is prostrating before the Lord, as ordained in the Qur'an: "Enter the gate prostate, and We shall forgive you your faults;" (2: 58) and prostration here means to shun the enormous deeds which are forbidden, which will ensure forgiveness of sins. Next, a nucleus must realize that the Kingdom of Allah will not be established by resorting to coercion; for, as Allah tells us in the Qur'an, "Let there be no compulsion in religion. Truth stands out clear from error: whoever rejects evil and believes in Allah has grasped the most trustworthy hand-out." (2: 256) He, the nucleus, further learns that the kingdom of the *taghoot* is founded on compulsion and terrorism: Allah delineates the difference between truth and error; between, on the one hand, the way of terrorism and coercion (i.e. the way of rebellions), wars raged by tyrants and dictators, those who have earned Allah's wrath and have gone astray; and, on the other, the way of free choice, where no coercion is used, the way of those on whom Allah bestows His grace, those who endeavor to erect the Kingdom of Allah, not taxing in that endeavor but themselves. The nucleus will then perceive that while the disbelievers have the *taghoot* for support, the believers have for friend and support Allah, the True King, the King of mankind, the Lord of mankind, full of kindness, the Merciful, the Compassionate, the Strong, the Proud, Who raises some, and brings down others; and the nucleus realizes that the path of the disbelievers leads from light to darkness, while the path of believers leads from darkness to light.

In this way the nucleus receives his training and enlightenment, until he is enabled to transfer what he has acquired to another nucleus; and whatever a nucleus has learnt must be tested through practice: a person who has not practiced bears a 'fail' score, for the devil will be his associate. An obedient nucleus, on the other hand, will learn through the fundamentals of religion, which we list again:

1. Allah forbids indecencies, such of them as are apparent and such as are within,
2. Allah forbids sin,
3. Allah forbids wrongful oppression,
4. Allah forbids associating with Allah that for which no warrant has been revealed, and
5. Allah forbids that you tell concerning Him that which you know not.

The nucleus will further study the conditions of piety and who are counted pious, who are the ones with understanding, who are well-guided, who are those who have surrendered, who have faith; who have gone astray, who are the disbelievers, who are evil-doers; what is transgression, and who are transgressors. And the wider one's scope, the more exacting the responsibility and the harder the progress – and the more rewarding.

The nucleus takes his duty quite in earnest, for he is aware of the mission he is to accomplish; and he neither cares for the slander leveled at him by many people, nor does he flatter or coax those above in the social ladder in hope of winning their favor. He does his utmost to fulfill his share, but he reflects before uttering his words. When he sees the most diligent in worship, he considers how to be equal to them, but when he faces the most vulgar he turns his attention inside to consider how he fares.

CHAPTER FIVE

Submission (to Allah)

A man who has submitted to his Lord is the nucleus who is equipped to establish the Kingdom of Allah in the earth; it is he who will bear the brunt of the great responsibility: that is commonly granted. But the question is who is a Muslim; what are his traits and what distinguishes him? Who are the real Muslims? All kinds of ideas exist about identifying the Muslim: there have been so many traits claimed, but no unanimity exists about the identity of a Muslim. For my part, I find that the right way is to refer to Allah's Words in the Qur'an, where we find:

"Abraham was not a Jew nor yet a Christian; but he was true in faith, and bowed his will to Allah's, which is Islam, and he did not join gods with Allah." (3: 67)

Or take the following statement of faith, made by Joseph, peace be upon him, as reported in the Qur'an,

"O my Lord! You have indeed bestowed on me some power, and taught me something of the interpretation of dreams and events – O You Creator of the heavens and the earth! You are my Protector in this world and in the Hereafter. You take my soul in death as one submitting to Your will, as a Muslim, and unite me with the righteous." (12: 101) It is submission on the part of Joseph.

Or take another,

"And who turns away from the religion of Abraham but such as debase their souls with folly? Him [Abraham] We chose and rendered pure in this world: and he will be in the Hereafter in the ranks of the righteous. Behold! His Lord said to him: 'Submit (to Me);' he said: 'I submit to the Lord and Cherisher of the universe.' And this was the legacy that Abraham left to his sons, and so did Jacob; 'Oh my sons! Allah has chosen the faith for you; then do not die except in the faith of Islam.' Were you not witnesses when death appeared before Jacob? Behold! He said to his sons: 'What will you worship after me?' They said: 'We shall worship your God and the God of your fathers, – of Abraham, Isma'il (Ishmael), and Isaac, – the One True God: to Him we submit; '" (2: 130-133) Abraham and his descendants announce here their submission [Islam].

The same was announced by Christ's disciples, as reported in the Qur'an:

"When Jesus found unbelief on their part, he said: 'Who will be my helpers to the work of Allah?' Said the disciples: 'We are Allah's helpers: we believe in Allah, and you bear witness that we are Muslims." (3: 52) In all the above 'Muslims' means: submitting to Allah.

And all the above is not different from what we read in the Bible, where Jesus, peace be upon him, says:

"My meat is to do the will of him that sent me, and to finish his work." (John, 4: 34) : It is the same declaration of submission.

Back to the Qur'an we read: "And say to the People of the Book and to those who are unlearned: 'Do you submit yourselves?'" (3: 20)

Also we find the Qur'an reporting Noah, peace be upon him, as saying:

"But if you turn back consider: no reward have I asked of you: my reward is only due from Allah, and I have been commanded to be of those who submit to Allah's Will." (10: 72)

Another verse of the Qur'an addresses believers in this way: "And strive in His cause as you ought to strive. He has chosen you, and has imposed no difficulties on you in religion; it is the cult of your father Abraham. It is he who has named you Muslims (submitting to Allah), both before and in this Revelation; that the Messenger may be a witness for you, and you be witnesses for mankind!" (22: 78)

The above verses show that the appellation 'Islam, or submission' was first used by Abraham, but submission as a doctrine had been adopted by each and every prophet after Abraham: Islam is not an unprecedented religion propounded by Prophet Muhammad, peace be upon him; it is rather the religion to which Abraham, peace be upon him, submitted, as did the rest of prophets. But what are the traits of a Muslim? Is he, as the imams say, the one who practices the five fundamentals of Islam, or is he somebody else? As ever, we seek light in the words of our Lord, so let's see how the Almighty defined Islam in the Qur'an. We find:

- "Whoever submits his whole self to Allah, and is a doer of good, has grasped indeed the most trustworthy hand-hold." (31: 22)
- "Your God is One God (Allah): submit then your wills to Him." (22: 34)
- "You turn to your Lord in repentance and submit to His Will;" (39: 54)

45

- "If anyone desires a religion other than Islam (submission to Allah), never will it be accepted of him; and in the Hereafter he will be in the ranks of those who have lost." (3: 85)
- "Say: 'O People of the Book! Come to common terms as between us and you: that we worship none but Allah; that we associate no partners with Him; that we do not erect, from among ourselves, lords and patrons other than Allah.' If then they turn back, you say: 'Bear witness that we at least are Muslims (submitting to Allah's Will).'" (3: 64)
- "Moses said: 'O my people! If you do believe in Allah, then in Him put your trust if you submit your will to Him.'" (10: 84)
- "But no, by your Lord, they can have no real faith, until they make you judge in all disputes between them, and find in their souls no resistance against your decision, but accept with the fullest conviction." (4: 65)
- "Those who submit their wills – they have sought out the path of right conduit." (72: 14)

It will transpire from the above verses from the Holy Qur'an that a Muslim is that who submits to Allah; and Allah is saying that the outcome of surrender to Him is freeing the individual from any other submission in the earth; Allah describes those who have broken free from being enslaved to people to be slaves of the Lord of people; describes those who submit as 'right-minded' [Arabic: *rasheed*]. Therefore, when we read the following question in the Qur'an: "Is there not among you any right-minded man?" (11: 78) we must understand it as meaning, 'Is there not among you a man who responds to Allah's law and submits to it?' And for evidence we have some verses from the Qur'an:

"For those who respond to their Lord, are all the good things." (13: 18)
"Those who listen in truth, be sure, will accept." (6: 36)

"Let them also, with a will, listen to My call, and believe in Me: that they may walk in the right way." (2: 186)
"But if they hearken not to you, know that they only follow their own lusts." (28: 50)
"You hearken to your Lord, before there come a Day which there will be no putting back;" (42: 47)

To sum up what has been said so far, Islam is submission: It is true that a believer must:
- Respond if commanded to perform prayer,
- Respond if commanded to perform pilgrimage,
- Respond if commanded to fast,
- Respond if commanded to pay the regular charity (*zakat*)
  – BUT,

That is only a small part of religion, nor does it comprise the fundamentals of Islam, as stated above; should one fail to perform any of the above deeds he would have committed a sin. As we stated, forbidding sin is one of the fundamentals of Islam; and it is commonly granted that prayer does distance one from committing the heinous sins. But if Muslims (those who have submitted to Allah) do wish to break free from the cave of political and cultural backwardness, let them break free first from the cave of the false religion which they endorse with their convictions, and let them endeavor to bring the religion they adopt to match that which they may find in the Scripture they hold in their hands. Now the only way to effect such a transformation is through the way propounded by the Almighty in such verses of the Qur'an as the following:
"And follow the way of those who turn to Me;" (31: 15)

But why this particular group, those who 'turn to Allah?' It is so because the one who 'turns to Allah' is truly well-guided: He would appeal to Allah in all his affairs, small or big; and this last point is made clear in the Qur'an, as we find in the following verse:

"Allah chooses to Himself those whom He pleases, and guides to Himself those who turn to Him." (42: 13) So submission is here the pivotal point. Not different from what we find in another verse from the Qur'an, where the Almighty says:

"There is for you an excellent example to follow in Abraham and those with him, when they said to their people: 'We are clear of you and whatever you worship beside Allah: we have rejected you, and there has arisen, between us and you, enmity and hatred for ever, – unless you believe in Allah and Him alone.'" (60: 4)

So who among Muslims today has responded and taken Abraham for an example that he follows?

The absence of the Qur'anic definition of the word 'submission' has caused chaos to the whole situation and upset the entire concept of true religion. That for one thing; for another, it has set Muslims in clash with several challenges, old and new, and in the cultural and political arenas. As a result, there have crept into the Islamic thinking concepts that are alien to religion; such foreign concepts have taken firm root in Muslims' cultural and intellectual consciousness, and in this way Islamic thinking has come to be false, having nothing to do with the Holy Qur'an; it has grown to be actually in conflict with it, and diametrically contrary to it. The outcome is something that anyone can see: that challenges and threats are looming everywhere, ready to attack any country that calls itself an Islamic country. Such efforts as are being made to bring the Muslims out of this quagmire are no more than ripples on the surface of a stagnant lake: you see how they go in one direction in the hope of getting out of the wilderness, and suddenly they find themselves in the midst of it again. All the attempts are failing since they do not address the real causes of the dilemma – it is true that thinkers, some religious-minded, are beginning to realize that there is a problem; but they perceive nothing about the nature of that problem, nor do they realize how to put right the present state, a state that has prevailed long enough – and so, some would resort to extremism, some would run after the *taghoots* of the earth, practicing the same terrorist ways their patrons practice. That has been so since they have wandered away from the right path: while they declare that Islam is the right solution, they do not notice that Islam is not adopted anywhere in the Muslim countries, nor does it have roots in their spirit – you do not suppose that those who lack faith can convey it to others! Seeking a solution under those circumstances is seeking a mirage, for allegiance to one's particular school of jurisdiction or race or nation is given precedence over allegiance to the Creator of the earth. And a Muslim is like a sheep in the flock, adhering to it, rather than to the Creator of the flock: it is a miserable state, when a Muslim has the gem in his hand and he is running after worthless trifles.

The trifle which man is running after at the moment is democracy.

In a state run by a 'democratic' system, man is an ass that is just given the choice of who will mount it – will your party be an *ikhwan* (the Muslim Brotherhood) or some other devil; and the poor ass marches to the ballot box to cast his vote, in which he states: "Let the so-and-so party mount on my back." And then, some years later, a party that has not yet ridden the ass will cry that reformation is badly needed, and so on.

Now since religion rejects all allegiances, national, racial, sectarian, or else, you find all efforts are made in vain, as long as the *taghoots* are in power, as long as wisdom has no adherents, and the one religion has been shredded into multiple religious schools to which various people subscribe; in the case of Muslims each extracting any verse he likes, out of context, to support his whims.

As for the ruler-controlled clerics, each utters his opinion, claiming it to be *shari'a's* (Islamic law's) view of life; that is what one watches in so many acrobatics, week after week, on the various channels.

The common man knows not who is to blame,
The ruler-controlled clerics?
The *taghoots* of the earth?
Or the colonial powers that occupy our lands?

And scholars have not given up writing their books, century after century, deeming such books to be a revival of the sciences of religion!

That is so, when Allah says in the Qur'an:

"Say to them: 'It [what befalls you] is from yourselves'" (3: 165)

But unfortunately, most people seem to have eyes that do not see, and ears that do not hear; they are like the cattle, or farther astray.

What Allah has revealed is one religion, not a multiplicity of religions; nor does Allah alter His religion. It is true at the same time that for each stage, and for any set of circumstances, there is a system that complies with its objective temporal conditions. If Christ's religion were Christianity, that would not have been accepted by Allah – his religion is Islam, submission to Allah. You may find evidence for this in his assertion on many occasions that he only did what pleased God. That is true too of Moses and all the prophets: though to each God prescribed a law that suited their particular circumstances, the religion of all was the same, the same in its essence and basic truth: and the purport of this is submission and obedience to what Allah ordains, to respond to Him, being the One God.

Let's now review the common terms between the People of the Book and others (see the Qur'an, 3: 64); we notice some points in those common terms which will shed light on the definition of the Muslim. We find that the Almighty Allah lays down specific conditions in that connection, namely:

Conditions of the common terms:
1. That we worship none but Allah; that we associate no partners with Him;
2. That we do not erect, from among ourselves, lords and patrons other than Allah.

We are commanded, if the People of the Book decline to act on the above conditions, to keep clear of them, affirming at the same time that we do submit to Allah according the above conditions. Now by looking more intently at these conditions we find that they fall under the general call of all prophets which is, according to the Qur'an:

"Serve Allah and eschew the *taghoot*." (16: 36)

Indeed, the kernel of Islam is surrendering to Allah, by worshipping only Him, and shunning idolatry – it is that the king, the president, the party, or any other authority other than Allah, is not held as man's referential entity.

So Allah has laid down a doctrine based on the well-known statement, "There is no god but Allah;" and one has subscribed to this doctrine if he submits to this proposition in its deep sense, and not in a superficial way as people repeat it five times a day without reflecting on it. Submission would imply that there is no lord of this universe but the Almighty, that there is no other party in the world, no matter how great it seems, entitled to subjugate me to it: that is Islam, and it is the freedom that a right-thinking person really seeks. To hold to that firm hand-hold (the hand-hold to Allah) is the essence of submission to Allah. The core meaning of that hand-hold, put in a nutshell, is to be found in the statement, "Serve Allah and eschew the *taghoot*." (The Qur'an, 16: 36) Not different from the other statement, "There is no god but Allah."

A Muslim nucleus realizes this quite well; he is fully aware of the two poles in existence: therefore he submits to no other gods other than Allah, nor does he associate any partners, no power in existence, no matter how great, to Allah. This however, leads us to a relevant question:

Allah has created this universe based on two poles, and made man is being pulled by one of the two poles, namely

<u>Allah</u>　　　　　or　　　　　the ***taghoot***

And man is given the choice to worship Allah or worship the *taghoot*; if he worships the latter, then he is labeled a non-Muslim (by not submitting to Allah), but is rather enslaved by a being who is, like the worshipper, himself a slave of Allah. Now it has been a problem for some who claim to be Muslims what is the way to deal with this latter pole who assumes the part of divinity and lordship in the earth.

What weapon should we use in resisting this latter pole? Is it to murder him, or to shun him and obey Allah? For an answer, let's refer once more to Allah's words in the Qur'an:

"Serve Allah ⟶ and eschew the *taghoot*." (16: 36)

Let's also recall what Abraham and his followers said to their people, as reported in the Qur'an: "We are clear of you and of whatever you worship besides Allah: we have rejected you, and there has arisen, between us and you, enmity and hatred for ever, – unless you believe in Allah and Him alone." (60: 4) When this is blurred, you find, as you see now, the *taghoot* proclaiming, "We believe in Allah," after he has made sure that Allah's religion has been distorted out of recognition; supported in that by the cleric (the imam) who sits in the lap of some *taghoot* of the earth.

It is crucial for better envisioning this situation to recite the following verses of the Qur'an that describe how an imam will announce, on the Day of Judgment, his breaking free from those who followed him:

"Then would those who are followed clear themselves of those who follow them: they would see the penalty, and all relations between them would be cut off. And those who followed would say: 'If only we had one more chance, we would clear ourselves of them, as they have cleared themselves of us.' Thus will Allah show them the fruits of their deeds as nothing but regrets. Nor will there be a way for them out of the Fire." (2: 166-167)

The way out is of course pointed out in the strategy set down by Allah, in the single word 'eschew' (see Qur'anic verse above), and not in any other approach. This simply means that a Muslim is forbidden from murdering the *taghoot*; nor is he to work for him, to serve in his army or to support him in any way. To eschew means that one behaves in the same way as a drop of oil dropped on a container of water: it would not mix with it in any way; and a Muslim may not associate with the *taghoot* in any way. This is of course so for good reason, a reason explained by the Almighty, too: Allah is telling a Muslim that once he shuns the *taghoot*, neither associating with him nor fighting him, the latter will collapse by himself: this indeed is what we have seen in the story of Moses and Pharaoh, for the latter fell down by himself, and Moses did not fight him.

In the same way, the Almighty commands his prophet Muhammad, peace be upon him, in these words:

"So break away [from the adversary] and withdraw from the idolaters." (15: 94)

He is commanded to break away with the *taghoot* and with all that work for him, even if they happen to be members of his family – the path of the *taghoot* is not that of Allah, the Lord of men and the King of men.

A Muslim nucleus realizes that exactly; he is aware that there are three types of men, in relation to Allah and the *taghoot*:

1. Those who eschew the *taghoot*, worship Allah and submit to him: this is the group who have broken away with the *taghoot*, and prostrated themselves to Allah, of their own accord.

2. Those who assume that both the sword and the sustenance are in the hands of the *taghoot*; that the ordinary man has no alternative but to succumb to him who has both sword and sustenance: this group will work for the *taghoot*, vindicate his concepts, seeking to maintain a balance between Allah and the *taghoot* (those who are reckoned powerless, and find it unavoidable to flatter the *taghoot*.)

3. Those who endeavor to murder the *taghoot*, with the intention of replacing him as the *taghoot* of the earth, to rule by the same doctrine he (the arrogant) used. What the *taghoots* of the earth are anxious to do at present is to reach their destinations by riding on the shoulders of the devout servants of Allah, while the Qur'an says of a situation like this:

"Do the unbelievers think that they can take My servants as friends beside Me? Verily We have prepared Hell for the unbelievers for their entertainment." (18: 102)

It is with this in mind that the *taghoots* of the earth hail national reconciliation.

A Muslim, however, turns to Allah in every issue, small or big, anxious and fearful in his search at all times for that which will be pleasing in the sight of Allah; he will deem Allah's law as above any other law; his life and death are in the name of Allah alone. Therefore, a Muslim nucleus, he who seeks right thinking, will view things from a perspective different from that of other people's: he will classify people in the way Allah classifies them; he realizes that some people claim to be believers when they are not, realizes that Allah calls such people as 'mischief makers' (the Qur'an, 2: 12). He is conscious that people are either submitting and doing what is good, or non-submitting, and making mischief. The nucleus perceives, too, the fine differences between a striving person, a patient person, and a fighter – what the True Lord has said about each, and the part He has given each.

This nucleus (the submitting nucleus, who prostrates himself to Allah, and shuns the major sins) knows well the difference between the most excellent goal (on the Day of Judgment) and the enjoyment of self-delusion (in this world); and therefore he will surrender to what Allah commands him, fulfilling the conditions for attaining the most excellent goal; his sole real concern lies in securing the pleasure of his Lord.

And when you set your goal as the best of goals, you will be sure to secure both goals (success in both this and the next worlds); while working for the enjoyment of self-delusion is transitory: it does not last long.

To clarify, a Muslim's yardstick is the Scripture of Allah, to which he always turns for guidance; it is there that he checks what Allah directs him to do, and he will readily respond to it and obey it (he willingly prostrates himself to Allah.)

But when some claim that a Muslim is he who declares the testimony of faith, who prays, pays the regular charity (*zakat*), performs pilgrimage, and fasts, their claim has nothing whatsoever with the way Allah defines a Muslim. A Muslim is that who turns to Allah in everything, small or big, submits to Him, and, apart from Allah, excludes all others from the right of dominating his life.

It is true, then, that Allah enacted for every nation a law and a doctrine that varies with the change of time; that He wills for every nation a different way; but Allah will not tolerate any compromising of his religion (Islam) which is founded on upholding the cause of Allah, and not any other's; never submitting to other lords in the earth – absolutely shunning them; and this is sure to secure triumph from Allah, for Allah never fails to fulfill His promise.

CHAPTER SIX

The Patient in Relation to the Nucleus

It has been said above that by placing man on earth, Allah willed the raising of the nucleus, for the nucleus is the basic building block of Allah's Kingdom. It follows from this that we have to be precisely clear about the features of this man who will erect this great structure. Indeed, the features of any structure must be decided in light of the nature of that structure. In the same way, Allah's Kingdom must have for its building block a man that is characterized by features that have been pinpointed by Allah, and the features derive from certain concepts. And so, I try now to go through those features, set by Allah for man to justify his inclusion in those who establish the proposed Kingdom.

The nucleus is a cell in a body; and the more this cell acquires knowledge and guidance, the better it is equipped to perform any function for the body, to serve the needs of the body, in accordance with the Qur'anic law, 'above everyone who is endowed with knowledge there is someone who knows more.' (12: 76)

Now patience is a precondition for the success of any action, small or big – that is because no matter how highly qualified one is, and no matter how talented or clever, when he embarks on the proposed work, unless he has perseverance and endurance, he will not accomplish the work, or he will do it incompetently; while Allah wants His Kingdom to be established in the best way.

Patience pertains to the character of man, and it is a hard thing to realize: therefore Allah encourages man to realize it when he says:

"And be steadfast in patience: for, verily, Allah does not fail to requite the doers of good!" (11: 115)

from which it will be clear that patience is a binding requisite if one has set out to attain any kind of target. And patience in the context we are about means that man must comply with the rules of architecture while he is working on the structure, that he only uses the specific building materials suitable for the work, and that he is punctual in abiding by the schedule set for the project. Now all the above is specified exactly by Allah, and man needs only refer to Allah's Scripture to find guidance about architecture, material, and time. He will also find the delay fine one will have to pay in case he has not finished the construction by the scheduled period, or in case his qualifications fall short of the ones stipulated in the contract. And man is accountable for the above conditions.

Men are examined against what had been inspired to their conscience, the true religion whose truth is reflected inside their minds, and as to what extent they have complied with it. Piety has not settled in man's heart except to the degree he will comply with its conditions and apply those conditions under all diverse circumstances. It is through real situations that truth takes root in the spirit and becomes the basis of perceiving Allah's will. Only then can the nucleus realize what he is bound to comply with, not heeding to what his desires or whims induce him to do: a nucleus is placed in the earth to act on Allah's will, which he perceives well, and acts in its light in real life situations, true to the precise system he finds in Allah's religion.

It is Allah who sent His messenger with the task of spreading guidance and the religion of truth, to the end that He makes it prevail over every false religion [see the Qur'an, 48: 28]. Therefore we say that the nucleus has relinquished his desires and whims, and proved to be steadfast in acting, at all times, upon the command of Him who created all things: he is indeed like the candle, burning to give light to those around it, so that no one remains in doubt about it.

It is this responsible behavior in actual situations that really characterizes the nucleus. See how the Almighty Lord describes the nucleus in the following verse of the Qur'an:

"Is then he who was dead in spirit and whom We thereupon gave life, and for whom We set up a light whereby he might see his way among men – [is he then] like one who is lost in darkness deep, out of which he cannot emerge?" (6: 122)

A nucleus is vividly aware that devils whisper unto their allies that they should involve believers in argument; but if the latter pay heed to them, they will be idolaters; and realizes, too, that to the unbelievers their deeds seem pleasing.

So what are the guidelines of patience as charted by the Lord; let's see what He says in the Qur'an:

"If you are patient in adversity and conscious of Him, and the enemy should fall upon you of a sudden, your Sustainer will aid you with five thousand angels swooping down. And Allah ordained this only as a glad tiding for you, and that your hearts should thereby be set at rest – since no succor can come from any save Allah, the Almighty, the Truly Wise." (3: 125-126)

The above is one of the verses in which Allah assures the man who will start working on the structure that Allah will support him with soldiers, though he cannot see them; that those soldiers will double the results of his efforts in building: that is promised man if he can show resolution.

That will take place if he shows dedication in his work of construction, for patience is the first test of a believer's faith; and the degree of his patience indicates the degree of his faith. We have a model here, when Ishmael was tested when his father was about to slaughter him, and the son said, 'Thou will find me, if Allah so wills, among those who are patient in adversity.' (the Qur'an, 37: 102) And as soon as Ishmael uttered this, Allah dropped that ordeal, for the purpose was to test his faith through the amount of patience, that is through the degree of his dedication; he did merit the other verse of the Qur'an:

"And most certainly shall We grant unto those who are patient in adversity their reward in accordance with the best that they ever did." (16: 96)

The nucleus realizes to whom belongs the right of judgment, keeping away from trespassing or detracting from the rights of Him Who created everything: he would not try to replace His judgment with any other's. He perceives what is right, adopts it, enjoins upon others to comply with what is right, and to have patience in keeping to what is right.

But words will never stand for experience, as experiencing the truth will illuminate the heart, even after death; so one will have his light glowing through layers over layers of darkness, and it will in this way revive all that is in life and imbue it with a new significance.

To have patience means to abide by Allah's commands, regardless of what obstacles may arise on the way, threatening to destroy the effort. We say that with reference to Allah's words when he says:

"All falsehood is bound to wither away." (17: 81)

Therefore, a nucleus stays true to the cause he has adopted until Allah's will in eliminating falsehood is fulfilled. And that class of people does merit to be called 'patient'.

But this does not come about without hardship, for man is hasty in his impatience to see the fruit of his effort. That is why you see man lose his patience sometimes, abandoning some of Allah's commands – that is shown in his attempt to slay the *taghoot*, forgetting the injunction of Allah, as we find it in the Qur'an:

"And endure whatever people may say against you, and avoid them with a comely avoidance." (73: 10)

"Await, then, in all patience your Sustainer's judgment, and pay no heed to any of them who is a willful sinner or an ingrate." (76: 24) And,

"Hence, remain patient in adversity – for, verily, Allah's promise always comes true." (40: 77)

Patience, then, is shown in constancy of dedication.

Some people get confused, in the course of affirming the right of both parties, in debates, to speak out, to criticize, to have their independent viewpoints, and to express them freely. They get confused, when discussing the rules of disagreement in the religious domain, about what is personal opinion and what is ordained religion. The outcome of this has been the prevalence of intellectual tyranny and cultural dogmatism; as displayed in extracting some verses from the Qur'an out of context, and twisting them to fit certain preconceptions; or giving them self-contradicting senses which are not comprehended by the public; the latter being, for one thing, ignorant of Allah's Scripture, and ignorant, for another, ignorant of Allah's laws in the universe. In consequence we have a long history of deplorable fanaticism, sectarianism, and radical extremism; all of which has led us to a deep abyss, as there is a real barrier between people and the Holy Qur'an. When I say this, my purpose is to do my share in helping Muslims to take the right attitude to the challenges that they encounter: it is not to reproach any particular individual; it is rather that we rally around the Holy Qur'an and all the good fruit it bears: the felicity, peace and mercy it has for all mankind.

Hence we repeat that Allah's commands are clear, enjoining patience and disobeying the *taghoot*. This goes to the point of calling man to accept to suffer physical and moral injury rather than concede to the *taghoot* – that has been actually practiced by Moses and his followers in their confrontation with Pharaoh, when the latter threatened, as the Qur'an tells us (as for example in 7: 127..; 20: 71; etc.) to cut off the hands and feet of the believers, to kill off their males and spare only the women; and to banish them. That is to say, Pharaoh was threatening with all forms of persecution, transgression against women, confiscating money, and corporal torture; and yet Moses' reply was that they would bear with patience whatever hurt Pharaoh would inflict on them. This shows that Allah did not warrant to the believers to kill Pharaoh; instead, he enjoined on them to have patience (dedication, perseverance); and of course Moses was true to Allah's direction; and the reward was that he was given support by his Lord.

From this we learn that the judgment concerning the conflict of believers and non-believers is definitely not what we witness today, not to settle the dispute through the sword, nor through slander.

We may consider in this connection the words of Shu'aib to his people, as reported in the Qur'an:

"Have patience till Allah shall judge between us and you: for He is the best of all judges." (7: 87)

It is past wonder that man should abandon the Best of judges and resort to the sword and to killing to be the arbiter between two groups. Judgment is due only to Allah: He and not man is the Judge. Even when man decides to withdraw from society and be isolated, he should do it according to a well-arranged and profitable method.

To have patience is ordained by Allah: it is not entrusted to certain individuals, so that only they are responsible for it while the rest of society can be free to forget about it as long as that group does what is due on it. We may consider in this respect the following verse from the Qur'an:

"And enjoin upon one another the keeping to truth, and enjoin upon one another patience in adversity;" (103: 3)

which asserts that these people enjoin upon each other to keep to truth, and enjoin upon each other to be dedicated and constant in that regard. There is nothing about succumbing to subjugation or weakness; it is rather taking a firm position.

Now truth is no more than what Allah's apostles have taught. Let's also note that the expression 'enjoin upon each other' is an imperative; it is a social duty, a kind of joint responsibility, missionary work within the community.

But it is unfortunate to notice how man has lost his confidence in patience in adversity – he regards it as a kind of weakness and poor self-assertion, while the Almighty tells us that patience is firmness of purpose (31: 17). And this mistaken approach to the meaning of patience has led to disagreements in the tactics and strategy of constructing both individual and society, and in establishing Allah's Kingdom. Let's remember that, as the Qur'an teaches us, "Allah does not change people's conditions unless they change that which is in their hearts." (13: 11) So let's consider what values and concepts we need to change in our society, by getting back to Allah's system, and let's check how each concept acts in our life.

Patience is then incumbent on each one of us – it is so because Allah has arranged things according to a specific succession: 'B' for instance is based on 'A', so that 'A' must be realized before 'B' can be realized. It is a comprehensive and integrated system, exactly as a house is built. In constructing a house, there will be digging, laying foundations, building walls, putting windows and doors in their places. Doors may not be put before laying the foundations, for if the order is reversed, the structure will quickly crack.

You do not paint walls before the walls have been built. And in every construction operation there are definite psychological, mental, and social factors to be realized. In some situations patience and *jihad* must be given priority, and in some situations fighting is right – for each approach there are appropriate terms, conditions and functions. Fighting may not be placed ahead of patience, for in this case the house will fall down into rubble. Patience is dedication and perseverance; it is the essence of submission, and jihad does not mean killing or fighting. Allah specifies who among people we may associate with, who it is unlawful to fight: the last are, as specified in the Qur'an, those who have not fought us for our faith, nor have driven us out of our homes (60: 8). Allah also defines, in the same verse, the kind of relationship with those who have not done the above mischief, a relationship of kindliness and justice. But there will be further down a full discussion of fighting and its conditions; and jihad and its conditions.

CHAPTER SEVEN

Allah's Balance

Viewing the Qur'an or Christ's words in the Bible would unfold a quite different picture from that held by Muslims on the one hand, or the followers of Christ on the other. What the present book tackles is the crisis of the current dispute in the Arab-Islamic circles, particularly in connection with the raging crises in the intellectual domain.

We need first to realize the difference between aggressive and vindictive criticism on the one hand, and constructive criticism which is based on evidence and proofs on the other: whenever we come across vindictive terms charging the adversary with being an agent, unbeliever, heretic, or the like, we should at once recognize that jargon for unfounded slander, unless the proofs and evidence are presented. For a relevant verse, we read in the Qur'an: "O you who believe! If any iniquitous person comes to you with a slanderous tale, ascertain the truth, lest you hurt people unwittingly and afterwards be filled with remorse for what you have done." (49: 6)

Having said that, I do realize that what I say on these pages will cause pain to some, but I invariably support what I say with evidence,
- From the words of Allah,
- The words of the messenger,

- Or the words of Christ.

I have tried my best to avoid all that is subjective impression, invariably providing evidence and proofs, from the Holy Qur'an for those who believe in it; and, for those who claim to follow Christ, I list evidence from the words of Christ himself, drawn directly from the Bible, from the prestigious version called 'red letters' (King James Version; Holman Bible Publishers, Nashville, Tn . Eyre and Spottiswood Publishers, London.)

And now, to proceed with our discussion, we may say that the basic balance of Allah's when dealing with His servants from the most ancient times is based on two poles or two scales; and the two scales are represented in the following values:

1. Separating from the opposite side
2. Absence of the Creator

1. Separating from the opposite side
It means detaching oneself from a society that has chosen to banish Allah from its intellectual system and in its everyday life. This is what we are commanded by the Almighty Lord when he says in the Qur'an:

"Therefore break away by virtue of what you have been commanded and turn away from those who join false gods with Allah." (15: 94)

And hence what Allah says elsewhere that we have in Abraham and his followers an excellent example (60: 4).

This directive has of course been observed by each and every one of the prophets, starting with the first and ending with the last. You will find the prophets abandoning their homelands, detaching themselves from their people. With this decisive step there was a crossroads, where the prophets followed one way, different from the others who have in practice, and not just in words, banished Allah from their life: when a people fail to comply with the cardinal principle of religion, that of forbidding idolatry, then detaching oneself from them is inevitable.

See how Jesus Christ calls the others dogs at times and swine at other times, as you see for instance in the following statement of his: "Give not that which is holy unto the dogs, neither cast ye your pearls before swine." (Matthew, 7: 6)

And, in practice, Abraham, peace be upon him, detached himself from his family, his father and his people. The same was done by Moses, Jesus, Noah, Muhammad and every one of the prophets, peace be upon them all.

Not one of the prophets dissented from that Divine law. Not one insisted on clinging to his people who had banished the Creator. On the contrary, the prophets abandoned their homelands, their families, including parents and children. They detached themselves or migrated in Allah's wide land. The prophets realized that oil does not mix with water; that if it does, then it has lost its characteristic quality. That one decisive quality was observed by the prophets, as commanded by Allah, and so they isolated themselves, in the same way that a drop of oil protects itself from dissolving in the surrounding water. That is so because piety will not be fulfilled except through separating from the others – hence the unanimously adopted motto of all the prophets, who proclaimed to their peoples, as the Qur'an reports:

"O my people, worship Allah! You have no god other than him;" (7: 8; among many locations)

Guidance of individuals and communities does not take place, does not even start, before this separation. That is so because Allah guides no one except he who turns to Him, and unless he takes Him as his reference and the light of his life. If one, on the other hand, sits in the *taghoot's* lap, though he goes to Mecca to shout, "I am at your service, my Lord; *I am* at your service!" but later returns to his *taghoot* to say, "I am at your service! I sacrifice my life and all I have to you," then he will be among those described by the Almighty in the following verse of the Qur'an:

"Allah does not grace with His guidance such as are false and disbelieving." (39: 3)

And now, having ascertained that all the prophets of Allah did separate themselves from, and detached themselves from, any authority at odds with the commands of Allah (by not submitting or responding),

We may ask: Have the clerics done at present what the prophets did?

Let's decide that in view of the actual reality.

Christ has said, "Behold, they that wear soft clothing are in kings' houses." (Matthew, 11: 8)

So, how is the Vatican Pope attired? Is he in soft clothing? Is he in the House of God or the kings' house? Or does he, like the sunflower, bend towards the sun wherever it moves?

Indeed, Christ did warn his disciples against that when he said,

"Take heed and beware of the leaven of the Pharisees and the Sadducees." (Matthew, 16: 6)

So are the Pope and the clergy sitting at the same table with the *taghoots* of the earth, sharing their principles and ideas? Or are they responding to the warning of Christ, peace be upon him? Do they negotiate with Allah's enemies in the name of national reconciliation and national interests, and similar slogans? Do Muhammad's followers do the same as Christ's followers do? Has the priest detached himself from the *taghoot* as commanded by Allah, as we read in the Qur'an:

"Worship Allah and eschew the taghoot." (16: 36)

Or in the other verse,

"Do not obey him: but bow down in adoration, and bring yourself the closer to Allah." (96: 19)

So has this separation taken place? Are the two bodies detached? Or are they merged into one body and one spirit?

Has man dissociated himself from the *taghoot*, or is he sitting in his lap, fanning him, and looking for his next command, to be rewarded with a turban, a chair, or a position in the ministry of religious affairs?

Have you seen the priests separate themselves and stand clear of those who do not obey Allah, in the way the prophets of Allah, one and all, did, to keep high the word of Allah? Or are the priorities confused, and the cards mixed up, so that man has ceased to differentiate the paper sent by Allah from the paper written by the priest?

Some Muslim scholars and clerics have noticed this detachment, though not its causes. They have started calling people to follow the messenger, but without realizing the issue of separation or its causes. Form has taken the place of content in their case, and people of this understanding assume that wearing or eating as the messenger did means that one has followed him and taken him for example. The clerics deluded the simple Muslim into thinking that religion has five fundamentals; they did not point out that it really starts with one point, the point declared many times in the Qur'an, "Worship Allah, as you have no [true] god but Him;" (7: 59).

You see that "Worship Allah, and eschew the *taghoot*," has been the motto of each one of the prophets. Religion today, on the other hand, consists of much delusion and imitation: a false religion that has no existence except in the minds of the ruler-controlled clerics, who disseminate it among others in the way an infection is disseminated.

And that goes on without any comprehension or perception, in a way that is described by the following verse from the Qur'an:

"He will place obscurity on those who will not understand." (10: 100)

They do not seem to realize that the essence of religion is giving allegiance to Allah, the Almighty, by submitting to him and accepting His commands, and by unequivocal detachment from parents, children, nationalities and countries in the way of Allah, until and unless they believe in Allah, in Him alone. This detachment, in the way Allah indicates, has not taken place, and the priests, one and all, exhort people to defend the *taghoot*, under the pretext of defending the nation or the country – that when Allah says,

"When angels take the souls of those who die still unjust against their souls, they say: 'In what plight were you?' They reply: 'Weak and oppressed were we in the earth.' They say: 'Was not the earth of Allah spacious enough for you to move yourselves away from evil?' Such men will find their abode in Hell – what an evil refuge! Except those who are really weak and oppressed men, women, and children – who have no means in their power, nor a guide-post to direct their way. For these, there is hope that Allah will forgive: for Allah blots out sins and forgives again and again." (4: 97-99)

Note in the above verses the expression 'unjust against their souls': injustice is trespassing any of the limits ordained by Allah. This brings us back to the critical point: breaking away with the opposite camp; for failing to break away with them is trespassing a limit imposed by Allah. Exactly how to distinguish and recognize vividly what it is that is commanded by Allah, and what it is that is commanded by the human who speaks in the name of Allah is all-important. Should he that speaks in the name of Allah banish Allah from his consciousness, and then, quoting from the above verses the admonition, "'Was not the earth of Allah spacious enough for you to move yourselves away from evil?' " should the cleric urge us and exhort us to defend the homeland, it becomes incumbent on us to dissociate ourselves from the cleric himself, for now he does not speak from Allah but speaks from his devil, that is when Allah's commands have been banished from his mind.

As long as the priest wears the mantle of Allah, but eats the bread of the *taghoot*, the first step in religion has not been realized.

2. Absence of the Creator
Banishing the Creator from one's intellectual plan used to be simple, direct and audacious. It was as the Qur'an reported one of the pharaohs of the earth to have asserted, "No god do I know for you but myself." (28: 38)

The situation is today more complex: what the tongue utters is at variance with what the body does. The absence of Allah from the equation can be witnessed in more than one form and more than one appearance – sometimes encased in gilded paper, sometimes in silver, so that the glamour of an idea is more important than the idea itself: a rotten idea may shine splendidly, hiding its rottenness.

A *taghoot* does not pose now as a proclaimed rival of Allah, as he did in the past; he now disguises himself in Allah's mantle, talks in His name, and leads people in prayer; he would also fast with the fasters and perform pilgrimage with the pilgrims.

And yet, the fact remains that behind all that he does not judge in accordance with what Allah has revealed; nor does he act in accordance with a verse from the Qur'an like the following,

"Judgment rests with Allah alone – and He has ordained that you should worship none but Him: this is the one ever-true faith; but most people know it not." (12: 40)

Instead of Allah's teachings we have slogans like 'people are rulers,' and terms like democracy and political parties. The relationship is quite thick with the person in authority who has the brandished sword, threatening to behead any opponent; no breaking away is visible, and the imam is there leading the whole congregation in prayer. The *taghoot* that stands with people in prayer is not unlike the person who announces separating state from religion; and that in blatant contrast with Allah's telling us that religion in its entirety is the state, that the purpose of religion is to establish the State of Allah – that is, to establish a state in the Name of Allah, adopting His terms and applying His law.

In this way Allah will be the King of men, the Lord of men; He and not the *taghoots* of the earth.

Indeed Allah was banished (and still is) from people's mental equation from the first moment of men's existence on the earth, from the moment Adam, peace be upon him, decided to go to the forbidden tree, forgetful of Allah's command. The good thing about Adam is that he confessed his sin, and so Allah forgave him. But his children have forgotten this experience of Adam – they no longer recognize the sin they commit, the sin of banishing the Lord from their equation: indeed man does not even notice that he has banished Allah from his mental equation, for he assumes that what he utters is the same as Allah has spoken.

Allah did warn us against this banishing of His law and its dire consequences, when He told us to choose one of the two rulers in existence, either Allah or one of the mortal rulers, whether this latter rules in the name of democracy or not. Once you accept the *taghoot* for ruler, you banish Allah; and, in the same way, once you take Allah for ruler, the *taghoot* will definitely disappear by itself from the chart set by Allah for His State. That is so because opposites cannot, philosophically, scientifically or logically, exist simultaneously and in the same place.

But so long as human societies fail to do what a drop of oil does when dropped in water, by not keeping the opposites separated one from the other – they will sink lower and lower in their intellectual chaos, and that has been the case for fourteen centuries.

We again refer to the Qur'an where we find an excellent example of detachment, and that is in the story of the Companions of the Cave, about whom the Lord says,

"Or do you reflect that the Companions of the Cave and of the Inscription were wonders among Our Signs? Behold, the youths betook themselves to the cave: they said, 'Our Lord! Bestow on us mercy from Yourself, and dispose of our affair for us in the right way!' Then We drew a veil over their ears, for a number of years, in the cave, so that they did not hear: then we roused them, in order to test which of the two parties was best at calculating the term of years they had tarried. We relate to you their story in truth: they were youths who believed in their Lord, and We advanced them in guidance: We gave strength to their hearts: behold, they stood up and said: 'Our Lord is the Lord of the heavens and of the earth: never shall we call upon any god other than Him: if we did, we should indeed have uttered an enormity! These our people have taken for worship gods other than Him: why do they not bring forward an authority clear and convincing for what they do? Who does more wrong than such as invent a falsehood against Allah? When you turn away from them and the things they worship other than Allah, betake yourselves to the cave: your Lord will shower His mercies on you and dispose of your affair toward comfort and ease.'" (18: 9-16)

The above servants of Allah chose to enter the cave and stay there, rather than to dissolve and merge into the others: that was the way truthful servants of Allah were to follow.

CHAPTER EIGHT

How the Prophets Viewed Things as an Integral System

Allah's system, prevailing everywhere in the world, is ordered according to a precise hierarchy; and a comprehensive cycle of succession binds that hierarchy as a whole. This succession was well understood by the prophets; moreover, they acted upon it faithfully; and that enabled them to perceive the system with all its links.

Now to approach this system, we need to be cognizant of two elements:
- Allah's Scriptures, and
- Allah's laws.

And the history and progress of Allah's prophets and messengers was based on Allah's laws on the one hand, and His Scriptures on the other.

Logically, taking out any link in a chain of events or concepts renders the whole chain useless and incomprehensible. And it will make such chain inoperative in the actual world. For illustration, let us take the arithmetic operations: to do a multiplication operation, we may not ignore adding, for that would not be conducive to getting any useful answer.

This simple fact is not realized by Muslims nowadays: they do not perceive that worshiping the *taghoot* is a breach or disruption of the complete chain in Allah's system. For instance, Muslims think that they alone are the Muslims in the world, and, consequently, they confine pilgrimage to themselves, forbidding it to others; insisting on that while the Almighty Lord says:

"Pilgrimage thereto [to Allah's House in Mecca] is a duty men owe to Allah – those who can afford the journey." (3: 97)

It is for all men, for Allah is not saying it is for the followers of Muhammad, peace be upon him, or upon Muslims.

Nor do people seem to heed Muhammad, peace be upon him, when he said:

"There is no preference for the Arab over the non-Arab except in how much either fears Allah."

Some do talk and write about religious pluralism, the urgency of exchanging opinions, the need for debate among the various religions; and yet,

What they actually do is to attribute their views to religions, and call those views religious plurality. Therefore, it is vital that we stress two points here:

1. There is nothing about Allah's religion like religious plurality; and,

2. Such plurality as exists in this global village, such a small place, is indeed a deluded plurality, having nothing to do with Allah's religion; and that is so no matter what you call the religion: Islam, Christianity, Judaism, Shiitism, Sunniism, Orthodoxy, Protestantism, Catholicism, or whatever.

What Allah's prophets called to was just a single religion, each prophet heralding the next, each supporting all the others. For man to be freed from this wilderness in which he is suffering, it is crucial that we pull out that false religion from the minds of people and replace Allah's truthful religion, which they actually hold in their hands as a written document.

For more elucidation of the above point, you may read the following verse from the Qur'an:

"Say [O Muhammad]: 'O mankind! I am an apostle of Allah to all of you, sent by Him unto whom the dominion over the heavens and the earth belongs! There is no deity save Him; He alone grants life and deals death!' Believe, then, in Allah and His apostle – the unlettered prophet who believes in Allah and His words – and follow Him, so that you might find guidance!" (7: 158)

Please note two pronouns in the above verse,
-   The pronoun 'I', in the clause 'I am an apostle of Allah to all of you;'
-   And the pronoun 'Him' in the expression 'and follow Him'.

It is important to note that – for if one fails to distinguish that the referent in 'I' is different from that in 'Him', two different parties, it may be said frankly that the present work is not for him.

See also the first call in the verse, " Say [O Muhammad]: 'O mankind! I am an apostle of Allah to all of you'": is it a call to one particular group? Or is it general? And then there will be some who insist on 'a general religion' and 'a group's religion'

See what Muhammad, peace be upon him, says:

"There is no discrimination between an Arab and a non-Arab except by God-fearing."

Read also the words of Almighty Allah in the Qur'an:

"Blessed is He Who sent down the Criterion to His servant, that it may be an admonition to all creatures." (25: 1)

So, to whom was the Criterion [Arabic: the *Furqan*] revealed?

Answer: To Moses, peace be upon him, as supported by the following verse:

"And remember We gave Moses the Scripture and the Criterion: there was a chance for you to be guided aright." (2: 53)

And when the former verse says, 'that it may be an admonition to all creatures,' is this general, or specific to a certain group?

And again, see what Moses, peace be upon him, says, as reported in the Qur'an:

"I will nevermore be a supporter of the transgressors." (28: 17)

But in spite of that, Muslims say: "Support your brother, transgressed against, or transgressor."

Of course they will try to argue at length about a special meaning of 'transgression,' ignoring in the meanwhile the meaning of the word [Arabic: *thalem*] as used in the Qur'an. The prophets called people, their people and all people, without discrimination; they did not try to give themselves any special privilege by affiliating with a certain nationality, a party, or denomination: such artificial affiliations were not in their dictionaries.

And now there is much talk about a world which is 'a global village;' but, at the same time, there is another call which belies the above when so many identify with a nation or a group that is different from anyone else's.

Such ambivalence was not there in the vision of the prophets: for their absolute allegiance was to Allah, the One God: they saw things quite vividly and unequivocally. They understood things for what they were, while their followers failed in this. One example of how vividly the prophets viewed things may be noted in a statement by Joseph, peace be upon him, as reported in the Qur'an:

"The command is for none but Allah: He has commanded that your worship none but Him: that is the right religion, but most men do not understand." (12: 40)

Religion is here linked by Joseph, peace be upon him, to the concept of 'the command is for none but Allah.' It is a conditional relation: confining command to Allah is the condition for right religion – it is not, as some commentators claim, the five 'fundamentals', prayer, fasting, etc.

How the prophets viewed things is uniform; they had exactly the same view, one after one, and from the same perspective: hence you note their invariable call, as reported in the Qur'an: "Worship Allah; you have no other god save Him;" (for example, 11:50, 61, etc.) Or they said, "Worship Allah and fear Him." (29: 16) Now prayer is not worship, as is commonly claimed, for we are told elsewhere in the Qur'an:

"Serve Me, and establish prayer for celebrating My praise." (20: 14)

Serving Allah is one thing in the above verse; and prayer is another thing.

As when you say 'John and Bill,' John is one person, and Bill is another; the pair are joined with a conjunction.

It is only the *taghoot*-controlled imams that would claim that John and Bill are one and the same person.

'Serve Me' means that you do what I want you to do every moment of your life.

What Allah wants is a long list of commands, starting with submission, and then dedication, and ending with emulating the way of the prophets and messengers of Allah, of course within the law of, "On no soul Allah places a burden greater than it can bear. It gets every good that it earns, and it suffers every ill that it earns;" (the Qur'an, 2: 286).

So how can Muslims have the right morality and legislation when they are pulled in every direction: having allegiance to the authority of the moment, to nationality, to the party, and allegiance to Allah – that when it is otherwise in Allah's system, as stated in His words in the Qur'an:

"Serve Allah, and eschew the *taghoot*." (16: 36)

To accept 'Serve Allah,' as the rule would not conduct us to Allah by itself; there is 'and', the conjunction that adds another imperative, 'eschew the *taghoot*.' To serve Allah and serve the *taghoot* at the same time will break the whole chain, an integrated and continuous chain that conducts a believer to Allah, and so it was comprehended by the prophets. Survey the whole Qur'an and you will not find a single prophet who did not uphold and realize this rule.

This is affirmed by the Qur'an itself, where Allah says, in the same above verse:

"And we assuredly sent amongst every people a messenger with the command, 'Serve Allah, and eschew the *taghoot*.'" (16: 36)

In application, you may refer to what Abraham admonished his people, as reported in the Qur'an:

"And Abraham: behold he said to his people: 'serve Allah and fear Him.'" (29: 16)

But what is God-fearing? How do we show we fear Allah?

Our source will again be the Qur'an, where you find ten conditions which, if you apply on a daily basis, then you are among the pious. Beyond that, all that is asserted by the ruler-controlled imams are delusions and false opinions that have nothing to do with religion. When I say that, I do not speak from personal opinion, but I refer you to the ultimate source, where you may search for the definition of the God-fearing.

In one verse of the Qur'an we read:
"Verily, this community of yours is one single community, since I am the Lord of you all: worship then Me alone." (21: 92)

You may note how in the above verse the expression 'this community of yours' follows a long chain of prophets and messengers: it is in reference to all of them that the Almighty says, 'your community.'

Another verse in the Qur'an has this to say:
".. spacious is My earth: therefore you serve Me." (29: 56)

What earth is mentioned here? Obviously, it is the *entire* earth.

In contrast, what is that land which Muslims claim to be the 'land of Islam'?

Further, we may refer to the following verse, where it reports Jesus as saying to his people:

"It is Allah Who is my Lord and your Lord; then worship Him. This is a way that is straight." (3: 51)

But, in contrast with this, mankind today worships the *taghoots* of the earth (the Devil), claiming at the same time that they are Muslim, Christian or Jewish.

Another verse teaches us:

"And you question Our messengers whom We sent before you; did We appoint any deities other than Allah, Most Gracious, to be worshipped?" (43: 45)

While men do take the political parties for deities that they worship, raising the party's motto above that of Allah. That some parties disguise themselves in Allah's mantle 'Hezbollah' changes nothing of this fact.

Allah's prophets sold their souls to Allah: After that it was impossible for anyone to enslave them, by persuasion or by coercion, to another deity. That is because they envisioned the situation in its entirety, and so no *taghoot*, no matter how dominant, succeeded in subjugating any single prophet. Allah helped His prophets realize this condition for they digested the Divine command fully, and they acted on it: they broke completely free from the *taghoot*, neither serving him, nor fighting him. They clung fast to patience, and upheld the banner of jihad: hence it was not possible for any one, save their Creator, to enslave them.

It is otherwise with present-day Muslims, who have one enslaver after another subjugating them, in such a way that slavery has become the primary trait of Muslims. It is so because Muslims have failed to comprehend the law of separation, and the Divine reply has been that a Muslim has come to be enslaved by the others. A Muslim has failed to capture or recapture how the prophets behaved, nor has he been able to infer the prophets' approach to the Qur'an – hence, he imagined that fighting against the *taghoot* was the only way to vanquishing him: opposite to the strategy of prophets; the prophets issued from darkness into light, while Muslims, Christians and Jews move from light into darkness; and when they adopt directions that are contrary to those of the prophets, they cannot reach the same destination the prophets reached. Bilal, the prophet's companion, did follow the way of the prophets, that of patience: he did not adopt the way of the stick and the carrot. He understood indeed that the weapon of patience was more potent than any that the human mind had devised: that all other weapons were no more than a spider's web when contrasted with this weapon – the Divine weapon is that of eschewing, contrasted with the human weapon, that of guns and bombs: Allah says that the mighty weapon is that of separation and patience (and that is giving volition), while man's weapon is that of the *taghoot* (and that is compulsion.)

The prophets understood well the fact expressed in the following verse from the Qur'an:

"Whatever beings there are in the heavens and the earth do prostrate themselves to Allah (acknowledging subjection) – with good-will or in spite of themselves: so do their shadows in the mornings and evenings." (13: 15)

Thus, Allah's messengers chose, willingly, to prostrate themselves to Allah; while other humans prostrate themselves to Allah by compulsion, as attested by Allah's letting the *taghoots* of earth have dominance over them.

And when Allah's prophets saw the verse in the Qur'an which says, "It is only the Devil that suggests to you the fear of his votaries: do not be afraid of them, but fear Me, if you have faith," (3: 175) they feared no material weapon, but they took refuge in Allah's invincible weapon: **DETACHING THEMSELVES**

They sought the support of patience and prayer to attain the utmost and invincible weapon.

Christ did indeed express the same notion, though in the tone of his age and doctrine, when he said:

"And fear not them which kill the body, but are not able to kill the soul." (Matthew, 10: 28)

And, as he also said,
"Love your enemies, do good to those that hate you." (Luke, 6:27)

When he says the above, Christ is not uttering it just for the sake of love: he actually realized that it was the invincible weapon which would completely eliminate the enemy. It was that Christ well understood such statement of Allah as the following, found in the Qur'an:

"Nor can goodness and evil be equal. Repel evil with what is better: then will he between whom and you was hatred, become as it were your friend and intimate. And no one will be granted such goodness except those who exercise patience and self-restraint – none but persons of the greatest good fortune. And if at any time an incitement to discord is made to you by the Devil, seek refuge in Allah. He is the One Who hears and knows all things." (41: 34-36)

But do Muslims have patience? Will they be granted good fortune from Allah? Their actual conditions are the answer. Muslims have lost the light which will show them the way to erecting the Kingdom of Allah, and that is when they failed to remember the rules laid down in the Qur'an.

The structure has its pillars, its terms and requisites, all of which are not within access of Muslims, not even in a barely minimal degree: since the baseline, which is detaching oneself. is not there, then the structure which is to be founded on that will not be feasible.

More unfortunately, Muslims do the opposite of what they are instructed to do, and the guidance which the prophets acted on. That is obvious enough once you analyze the statements common in Muslim communities versus those uttered by the prophets: What you will discover is a really thick wall separating the first set of statements from the latter; the Muslims' way and that of the prophets share no more than the name. It is true of present-day Muslims the following words of the Almighty's in the Qur'an:

"Their similitude is that of a man who kindled a fire; when it lighted all around him, Allah took away their light and left them in utter darkness, and they have lost true direction. So that they could not see. Deaf, dumb and blind, they will not return to the path." (2: 17-18)

So is it ever possible to guide someone who did light a fire for some time, and then Allah took away his light and left him in darkness! It is true of them, again, what is said in the other verse:

"To those who reject Our signs and treat them with arrogance, no opening will there be of the gates of heaven, nor will they enter Paradise, until the camel can pass through the eye of the needle: such is Our reward for those in sin." (7: 40)

Such darkness as described in the above verse I detect in the discourse of intellectuals, for I see their base intentions demonstrated in every utterance of theirs; and I remark the wide chasm between what Allah teaches and what the intellectual believes. Some Muslim intellectuals, for instance, call for a separation of religion and politics, and find the calamities of Muslims to emanate from mixing up religion with state, while Allah tells us that Allah's Kingdom must be erected in the earth, and that means a pairing of religion and state.

Man is bound in fact to admit, as Adam did before, that he has lost the way, to admit that he has wronged himself. That is the first step, for to recognize the problem is the key to its solution. And that was clear to Moses' followers, as reported in the Qur'an:

"The people of Moses made, in his absence, out of their ornaments, the image of a calf, for worship: it seemed to low: did they not see that it could neither speak to them, nor show them the way? They took it for worship and they did wrong. When they repented, and saw that they had erred, they said: 'If our Lord have not mercy upon us and forgive us, we shall indeed be of those who perish.'" (7: 148-149)

But it is deplorable to note that the followers of both Moses and Muhammad have regressed to taking the calf for worship, assuming that the lowing it gives out betokens that it is a mighty being. But it is otherwise as Allah teaches us: that the weapons we see, nuclear and whatever, are like the calf that emits lowing, but has no power to guide; it will rather lead astray. So will someone ever realize that this calf will not lead to the way of Allah? Muslims are under the delusion that if they possess weaponry they will attain glory. But do not they see that the Soviet Union had enough military power to destroy the earth, several times over, and yet it collapsed. And so will the other governments of the earth once they ripen enough.

Man has violated the covenant between him and Allah, the contract summed up in the following command in the Qur'an,

"Do not take other than Me as disposer of your affairs." (17: 2)

In contrast, the prophets refused to have a covenant with the *taghoot's* kingdom. They severed all relations with any *taghoot* kingdom, while other humans have signed for a union, a quite unlawful one, with the *taghoot* governments of the earth.

Most vividly did the prophets and messengers of Allah choose their allegiance, and they never lost sight of it; and equally vivid were they about who they should dissociate themselves from. In this they realized the vital principle in religion, that of giving allegiance to Allah, and dissociating themselves from the *taghoot* and his minions. And hence

Allegiance   and   dissociation

Are

the key to change.

What we witness at present is that man has not changed that which is in his soul, for his allegiance remains to the *taghoot*; and so Allah does not change the circumstances of his life. The change in one's soul will come about in dissociating himself;

that the dissociation is not taking place means that the union is standing, that what mankind is complaining of, terrorism, will go on – for one of the results of man's failure to end the union with the *taghoot* is terrorism, which may go by other names like struggle, revolution, resistance, or any other appellation.

And so Muslims would like now to believe in the Compassionate and the *taghoot* at the same time, while Allah makes of them two incompatible entities, having no common ground, in either time or space.

And the world's ignorant group, the so-called scholars of the Muslim *ummah*, would go on suggesting new unions time after time, a new marriage without a prior divorce – and the result is the universal chaos and mischief in all corners of the world. Therefore, let me find my solace in the following prayer which Joseph, peace be upon him, uttered, as the Qur'an reports:

"O my Lord! You have indeed bestowed on me some power, and taught me something of the interpretation of dreams and events – O You Creator of the heavens and the earth! You are my Protector in this world and in the Hereafter. You take my soul at death as one submitting to Your will as a Muslim, and unite me with the righteous." (12, 101)

The righteous are of course those who give their allegiance to Allah, and not to the governments of the earth.

CHAPTER NINE

Another Perspective on the Concept of Jihad

Will Durant says, "For words are to thought what tools are to work; the product depends largely on the growth of the tools." (*The Story of Civilization*, Vol. I, page 71)

Over the past centuries, the concept of jihad has been identified in the human mind with the concept of fighting, so intimately that fighting is now taken to be *the* jihad. Therefore, what I shall be trying to do in the present chapter is to define jihad with reference to the Holy Qur'an; and then I define fighting. Last, I point out the points of similarity and points of dissimilarity between these two concepts.

Confounding the two concepts has resulted in grave consequences for the 'Muslim Ummah': so many crimes have been committed in the name of jihad; groups of murderers have been called *mujahids* 'jihad doers' – how far from truth!

A certain poet has described this situation in a couplet which says:
He deludes himself into calling his robbery and oppression a holy conquest: such a gross misnomer!

The truth of the matter is that a careful and informed study of the Holy Qur'an will reveal that there is not a single proof that jihad is fighting. My effort will be directed towards following up this concept wherever it is used in the Holy Qur'an, to reveal its truth, and to remove all the layers of dust that have been gathering on it and encrusting it.

The Concept of Jihad in the Qur'an:

The word 'jihad' has been encumbered over the years and for such a long time with meanings that have nothing to do with the word, neither in its linguistic nor its Qur'anic usages. The original sense of the word as 'striving' has been overlaid with a call to fighting and war – that had come only through the surmises of some people, but it descended like a disease across the generations. Real jihad was pinpointed by a most truthful source, the honest Messenger Muhammad;a man asked him: "O Messenger of Allah, what jihad is best?" and he answered: "To say the truth to a tyrannical ruler." (Al-Tabarani, *Al-Mu'jam al-Kabir*, Vol. 8, p.282)

And yet, it is to the Holy Qur'an that one must refer in order to bring out the pure and unadulterated meaning of jihad, in order to preserve the intellectual purity of every caring (submitting) Muslim, so that no misguided practices may lead him astray.
Jihad is striving to do good deeds, with a view to erecting Allah's Kingdom in the earth. To attain such target, we need first to be cognizant of guidance from Allah; and also to be acquainted with the way followed by the prophets and messengers, and their followers who walked in their steps. Let's now see how the word jihad has been used by the Almighty Allah. In one instance He says, as we read in the Qur'an:

"If they [either of your parents] strive [Arabic: *jahadaka*] to force you to join with Me in worship anything of which you have no knowledge, do not obey them." (29:8)

Where Allah calls the parents' endeavor to divert their son or daughter from Allah's way a 'jihad'; and in response, the Lord commands the son or daughter to decline from obedience: jihad is not murdering, for murdering is not striving, but a 'jihad'.
And generally speaking, killing does not mean 'striving': not in any language in the world; the reader may ascertain that for himself by checking in any dictionary.

In another verse of the Qur'an, we recite,

"O Prophet! Strive hard against the unbelievers and the hypocrites, and be firm against them." (66:9) He is not saying 'kill them'.

Elsewhere we recite in the Qur'an:
"Therefore, do not listen to the unbelievers, but strive against them with the Qur'an, with the utmost strenuousness." (25:52)

What we have above is pointing out by the Almighty Allah that to disobey is a jihad; and to keep aloof and at a distance from unbelievers and hypocrites is a jihad. There is not even any mention of fighting. The point may be further expounded, and the concept may be comprehended better, by looking at the way of Abraham, and at his endeavor.

But why Abraham, peace be upon him, and not any other prophet?

It is so because the Messenger, and all the other messengers, followed in the steps of Abraham, peace be upon him. That is how we understand the following verse in the Qur'an (reporting Allah's choice of Abraham):

"I will appoint you a leader for mankind!" (2:124)

Now Abraham detached himself from his people, and moved away from them. They tossed him towards the fire, but he abstained from fighting them. In this, Abraham was complying with the words of the Almighty:

".. striving [Arabic: performing jihad] in the way of Allah, and never afraid of the reproaches of such as find fault." (5:54)

It may be observed in the above verse that we have 'striving' versus 'being afraid of such as find fault': nothing about fighting.

It is jihad encountering reproach.

To disbelieve in the *taghoot*, and to separate oneself from a community that does not obey Allah, to abandon such community, is something that requires resolute striving. Such moving away and jihad will result in some reproach, oppression, hardship and sacrifices: all forms of afflictions that Abraham, peace be upon him, had to suffer in his jihad.

Similarly, Christ was mindful of what his disciples would undergo in their endeavor to train the nucleus, and this latter would be erecting Allah's Kingdom. That is clear in his warning to them: "Behold, I send you forth as sheep in the midst of wolves: be ye therefore wise as serpents, and harmless as doves. But beware of men: for they will deliver you up to the councils, and they will scourge you in their synagogues; and ye shall be brought before governors and kings." (Matthew, 10:16-18)

What Jesus taught his disciples on sending them are the rules of jihad, but fighting is nowhere to be found among his teachings. And again we refer to Abraham, the leader who was followed by Allah's messengers. Muhammad, peace be upon him, was commanded in his turn to follow in the steps of Allah's messengers and prophets: we recite in the Qur'an:

"Those were the prophets who received Allah's guidance: copy the guidance they received." (6:90)

If we make a full repertory of the prophets in the Holy Qur'an, we find twenty four prophets and messengers mentioned; and each one of them said to his people:

"We shall certainly bear with patience all the hurt you may cause us. For those who put their trust should put their trust in Allah." (14:12)

It may be noted that not in a single prophet's or messenger's plan was any intention of murder or fighting, for killing is governed by rules and conditions: about that we read in the Qur'an:

"Take not life, which Allah has made sacred, except with right and by law." (6:151)

The same expression is used in 17:33. That 'right' is the truth mentioned in another verse:

"The messengers of our Lord did bring the truth." (7:43)

As for the word 'kill' and its derivatives, we find it mentioned 170 times in the Holy Qur'an, but not once in connection with jihad. However, fighting will be elaborated further down, when we come to a discussion of Allah's Law.

The *Mujahed* (jihad doer) and the Patient

We read in the Qur'an the following words of the Almighty's:
- "Did you think that you would enter Heaven without Allah testing those of you who fought hard in His cause and remained steadfast?" (3:142)

- "Or do you think that you shall be abandoned, as though Allah did not know those among you who strive, and take none for friends and protectors except Allah, His Messenger, and the community of believers? But Allah is well-acquainted with all that you do." (9:16)

See in the above verse how jihad means that you strive in spreading Allah's religion, that you train another person to be himself a worker in the way of Allah, or be patient (holding fast the Allah's cause): there is no inkling in it about killing or fighting.

- "And We shall try you until We test those among you who strive their utmost and persevere in patience; and We shall try your reported mettle." (47:31)

It will be noted how doing jihad and patience are invariably linked together; and jihad includes striving with one's property and with one's person: with one's person because one's welfare and life will be in peril – we have seen how a *taghoot* will fill his jails, and will have so many buried in mass graves. That about striving with one's person. As for striving with one's property, it is so because a worker will spend freely to shelter those who have been persecuted in the way of spreading Allah's religion: hence striving with property and person.

- "Not equal are those believers who sit at home and receive no hurt, and those who strive in the cause of Allah with their goods and their persons. Allah has granted a grade higher to those who strive with their goods and persons than to those who sit at home. To both parties Allah has promised good: but those who strive He has distinguished above those who sit at home by a special reward." (4:95)

The above verse must suffice to untangle the whole problem – for if jihad meant fighting, there would be no difference between a home-sitting person and one doing jihad: it is an established fact in Islam that the one who fails to fight when fighting is enjoined, he is an apostate. A believer is bound to sever relations with such a person, and to detach oneself from him: that is established in the Qur'an. And one may also refer to the story of the three companions of the Prophet who failed to participate in a certain battle (see details about that further down.) On the other hand, in the above verse we have: " To both parties Allah has promised good," which would be impossible to apply to the sit-at-home if it were a command to fight, since fighting is a personal obligation on each and every eligible believer; and that is a quite decisive evidence. Jihad, however, is enjoined collectively; i.e. if done by a sufficient number, the others are free not to perform it. So may Allah guide us to what is right and true.

The Almighty Allah distinguishes between two groups of nuclei: the first group is that of *'mujahids*, the jihad performers'; and the second group is that of the patient. Each He distinguishes with characteristics and grades. In more than one location, Allah mentions the *'mujahid'* as one type and the patient as another:

"without Allah testing those of you who did jihad and the patient." (3:142)

A *'mujahid*, i.e. a jihad doer, is a person who is anxious and eager to do much more than is enjoined on him personally; he works with others to train patient and *mujahid* persons; he strives to do good deeds; and he undertakes what such efforts will entail, in the way of banishment, immigration, or material loss; and he gives refuge to those who have had to leave home in the way of similar endeavors. About that we read in the Qur'an:

"Those who gave them asylum and aid – these are all friends and protectors, one of another." (8:72)

The very trait *'mujahid'* denotes the willingness of such individual to sacrifice his life or welfare for the sake of the noble cause, or to spend out his wealth for that, or may be both. It is he who accepts to undertake, not waiting for any other, the bearing of a collective commandment.

A patient person, on the other hand, is one who is content to do what is personally enjoined on him: he does go ahead in doing what he is bound to do, offers his wealth, sacrifices his life if that is required of him – but he will not train another nucleus to share the burden; hence he is called a sit-at-home or a patient person.

All this may be illustrated from the striving of Christ: he strove and trained the disciples; and these latter bore the cause in their turn, following in his steps: and he also trained and taught others (the patient) who did not take part in spreading the message, nor endeavored in enhancing the cause of erecting Allah's Kingdom. Jihad is then to forfeit everything granted by Allah: offering one's property, soul, home, land, and family, in the way of erecting Allah's Kingdom in the earth. A person who does jihad will start, as Abraham did, by breaking away with the *taghoot*, detaching oneself from him, but without fighting him; striving strenuously and diligently to expand the circle of those who are devoted to erecting Allah's Kingdom. That is the part of a *mujahid*; and his reward with Allah is an immense one, for he submitted an utter submission to the commands of Allah – first by detaching himself, and next by offering all he had to the Cause of Allah. Here is a relevant verse in the Qur'an about that:

"Say: If it be that your fathers, your sons, your brothers, your mates, or your kindred; the wealth that you have gained; the commerce in which you fear a decline; or the dwellings in which you delight – are dearer to you than Allah, or His Messenger, or the striving in His cause – then wait until Allah brings about your decision: and Allah does not guide the rebellious." (9:24)

What we have here in Allah's words is a pinpointing of the obstacles that will stand in the way of a jihad doer. We do have a vivid example in the prophets: how they turned from their fathers (Abraham), sons (Noah), their wealth and homeland (Moses and Muhammad), may peace be on them all; and so did their followers who left behind their homelands and strove in the cause of Allah with great devotion.

A patient person (the complying person) is one who does good to himself alone: he does not contribute any substantial effort for the training and consolidating of the nuclei who erect Allah's Kingdom. A patient person does disbelieve, the same as a *mujahid* does, in the *taghoot*; he has withdrawn, taking his own way; he does accept the outcome of his disbelief in the *taghoot*. In short, he has achieved one good point, disbelieving in the *taghoot* and accepting whatever consequences may follow upon his disbelief in him – but without enduring the toilsome effort involved in erecting Allah's Kingdom. To further distinguish between the two types, we may say that a *mujahid* has effected a change in himself, and he strives to effect a change in the community as well. A patient person, on the other hand, is one who has effected a change in himself, but makes do with that achievement. No wonder then that Allah grants a *mujahid* a higher grade than a patient person, and guarantees the former an outcome different from the latter. In His words in the Qur'an:

"Not equal are those believers who sit at home and receive no hurt, and those who strive in the cause of Allah with their goods and their persons. Allah has granted a grade higher to those who strive with their goods and persons than to those who sit at home. To all Allah has promised good: but those who strive He has distinguished above those who sit at home by a special reward. Ranks specially bestowed by Him and forgiveness and mercy. For Allah is Oft-forgiving, Most Merciful." 4:95-96)

Let us pay attention to the expression, 'To all Allah has promised good;' which promises good outcome to both the jihad doer and the sit-at-home; and then recall the Messenger's handling of the situation in connection with the Tabuk campaign, where three Muslims failed to come forth with the other fighters. He commanded the rest of community to keep away from them; while they stayed in the midst of the community, no single soul would utter a word to them, no one would deal with them, not even their relatives, or their wives. It seemed to them that the earth, for all its spaciousness, was constrained, and their very souls were straitened for them; and they perceived that there was no fleeing from Allah but to Himself; then Allah turned to them with forgiveness. All this is recorded in the Qur'an (9:118). The idea here is that if jihad were fighting Allah would not say of those who do not take part in jihad, 'To all Allah has promised good.' Here is then a proof drawn from the Qur'an, and another drawn from His Messenger, both demonstrating that jihad is not fighting: but Allah suffices as an Observer and as a Witness.

The sit-at-home are those who are content to do what is enjoined on them, not endeavoring to produce other persons that do the same, though they do sever relations with the disbelieving party. Such persons are called sit-at-homes, and granted by Allah a lower degree than the jihad doers.

Jihad in the Cause of Allah and Jihad for Allah
Allah distinguishes between two kinds of jihad, jihad in the cause of Allah, and jihad for Allah: there are basic differences between these two kinds of jihad, in the amount of jihad contributed, and in the route each kind follows:

Jihad in the cause of Allah: it is jihad in teaching how a nucleus should be trained, in training individuals to follow the way of the jihad doer. We have an example in Christ, who taught the disciples how to disseminate Allah's message, how to promote His religion, fearing none but Allah. Jihad in the way of Allah will involve a willingness to sacrifice one's wealth and/or life; a readiness to immigrate and endure persecution and physical and moral privation. A *mujahid* in the cause of Allah may well have to undergo certain hardships, all indicated by Allah: thirst, fatigue, hunger, treading paths that will raise the ire of unbelievers, or receiving injuries from enemies. Allah describes a person who endures one, some, or all of the above as fulfilling the good deed of a *mujahid* in the cause of Allah. So let's recite the words of the Almighty about that:

"Because nothing could they suffer or do, but was reckoned to their credit as a deed of righteousness – whether they suffered thirst, or fatigue, or hunger, in the cause of Allah, or trod paths to raise the ire of the unbelievers, or received any injury whatever from an enemy: for Allah does not suffer the reward to be lost of those who do good." (9:120)

We have a good summing up of deeds and afflictions of the sort described above in the life of the Messenger and his companions in Mecca, then in their immigration to Medina.

Jihad for Allah: This kind of jihad does also involve striving for acquiring the principles of erecting Allah's Kingdom, acquiring an understanding religion; it also involves a readiness to offer the necessary effort in the way of heeding and obeying the commands of Allah. Here also there is the unavoidable conflict inside the individual for taking difficult decisions.

A careful study of the verses in the Qur'an pertaining to jihad will vividly reveal that in none of those verses is killing implied in jihad: they are quite different concepts; different in time, in place and in aim. Jihad, both in the cause of Allah, and for Allah, is a striving and enduring of hardships for Allah's command to be predominant in the earth; and jihad, in either of its two types, is the endeavor undertaken by an individual (in submission and dedication) for the erection of Allah's Kingdom in the earth. A *mujahid* is an individual who leads the way, who accomplishes more than others, and stops at no effort to achieve more. If we imagine a *mujahid* 'a jihad doer' as one who has begotten many children, then a patient individual is a barren person, who has no children at all: he is content to save his own soul. Abraham did great jihad when he was tossed in the midst of the fire, but Allah saved him from it. He did merit the promise of Alalh, "And those who strive in Our Cause – We will certainly guide them to Our Path." (29:69)

Abraham did set the example for all later poets to follow; and Allah links jihad to faith, for He says:

"Only those are believers who have believed in Allah and His Messenger, and have never since doubted, but have striven with their belongings and their persons in the Cause of Allah: such are the sincere ones." (49:15)

We have above a group of believers who obey Allah and His Messenger; who have no affection in their hearts for any one who adopts a hostile attitude to Allah.

Jihad starts in one's soul, where one is required to effect a change; and from there he sets out endeavoring to effect a change in society. Once both kinds of change have been accomplished, the relief mentioned by Allah will definitely come – the relief we read about in the following verse,

"Verily, with every difficulty there is relief." (94:6)

The difficulty that a *mujahid* suffers will be followed by relief, in both this world and in the Hereafter. Jihad, which is doing good deeds, will be rewarded with high grades in the Hereafter; and viceroyalty in the earth will follow upon the disappearance from the earth of the *taghoot* network which dominates at present.

The central point perhaps about the concept of jihad is its aim: for its aim is not the defense of self, home, or family – it is solely for laying the foundations of Allah's Kingdom, something which we humans have originally been created to establish; not in the way we wish it to be, but in the way Allah wills it to be – for homes, clans, or families are not a believer's protector. Allah is the protector, and anyone else who claims to be so is an intruder or imposter.

The major type of jihad, as described by Allah, is a dedication to apply Allah's commandments, to disobey and cut off relations with the unbelievers. So we may ask now: Is our society a *mujahid* society, according to the above formula? And is the imam we see in the mosque a *mujahid*? The rule for distinguishing jihad comprises five terms:
1. Showing firmness to unbelievers,
2. disobedience,
3. detaching oneself,
4. immigration, and
5. not taking unbelievers for protectors.

Which of the above five terms, one would wonder, is true of the imam? Or true of the Pope who is seated on his throne in Rome? It is the *taghoot* who is the ally of the imam and the Pope; neither have cut off relations with the society; neither of them has migrated, nor shown firmness to unbelievers: on the contrary, they show roughness to ordinary people, and call that strictness in the Name of Allah. Is either of the above two among those who do jihad in the Cause of Allah?

By scanning the Qur'an for the word 'jihad' and its derivatives, we find it mentioned 41 times, in nineteen chapters. But in none of the 41 locations does the word indicate fighting, as was decisively demonstrated above; and as will be more thoroughly and systematically demonstrated in the next chapter, which deals with fighting, its causes and conditions. Indeed, Allah sets for fighting and killing strict conditions, without which they are forbidden.

But if there is not a single proof or even a hint that fighting is synonymous with jihad, who are those who claim to be Muslim fighting for? That when the Messenger said, addressing a family of believers: "Be patient, Yaser and his family; we shall meet, you and I, in Paradise."

To conclude, if viceroyalty is the fruit of jihad in the Cause of Allah, we all realize that we are not striving in the way of Allah as is required of us. It is right, then, that Allah lets the *taghoot* trample us down, and many a *taghoot* have succeeded each other, sitting over our shoulders, for fourteen centuries. No victory will be granted us by Allah unless we uphold His Cause, and unless we erect the foundations of His Kingdom through exertion and through keeping away from what He forbids. A telling verse from the Qur'an is this:

"O you who believe! If you will aid the cause of Allah, He will aid you, and plant your feet firmly." (47:7)

To ascribe to the word 'jihad' the sense of fighting, without any evidence or proof, is flagrant fabrication, with nothing to support it from Allah's Scripture. One must be warned of such fabrication with this verse from the Qur'an:

"Those who ascribe false things to Allah, will never prosper." (16:116)

In this we perceive what is now causing the failure of Muslims.

CHAPTER TEN

The Concept of Fighting and Its Role in Allah's Kingdom

While discussing the concept of jihad I indicated briefly that jihad neither by denotation nor by implication meant killing, that the two concepts were quite independent from each other: each having its own sense and function. In the present chapter I discuss: How? Where? When? And why killing may take place?

The word 'to kill' or 'to slay' was used for the first time by Adam's first son, Cain, when he was about to kill his brother, Abel; and the latter did not defend himself, but said, as reported in the Qur'an:

"If you stretch your hand against me, to slay me, it is not for me to stretch my hand against you to slay you: for I do fear Allah, the Cherisher of the Worlds." (5:28)

It may be noted about the above situation how the former acted by the dictate of his desire, while the latter adhered to the conditions of piety, the conditions reported in the Holy Qur'an, as well as in Christ's commandments, as reported in the Holy Bible: there is no difference between the two sources.

In the event involving Adam's two sons, Allah is indicating that to slay another human being is not permitted, even in self-defense; that killing is unjust, a transgression of the limits

105

ordained by Allah: hence killing has been forbidden us by Allah; He warns us from committing such a deed.

By referring to the Qur'an, and by a careful survey of the verses that handle the concept of killing, we find that this deed is subject to so many conditions and restrictions – it is certainly not the reckless killing that we witness nowadays. Allah has set a whole system for killing, with full details concerning the act of killing, the fighter, the conditions for killing, its time and place – indeed, the laws concerning killing are most solemn, and the limits are most strict, so that a Muslim (who submits to Allah) may not trespass them. Killing is forbidden in most situations, but, on the other hand, it is enjoined under certain circumstance.

1. When Is Killing Enjoined on A Believer? (A personal duty)

Fighting is enjoined if and only if the following five conditions are met; conditions which one, if he be among those graced with Allah's bounty, can trace in the Holy Qur'an:

1. The existence of Allah's Kingdom (according to the terms set by Allah and not by the *taghoot*)
2. That an enemy is the side that starts the belligerence
3. That fighting is embarked on in the cause of religion, and not for territory, wealth, authority, etc.
4. That fighting continues
5. That fighting is carried out by believers, God-fearing people: it is this class of people who are addressed in the commands of fighting.

A believer is: a person who submits, a dedicated person, who has expelled from his heart any affection for those who take an aggressive attitude to Allah; keeping his distance from this latter. Let's read about that in the Qur'an:

"Fear Allah, that you may prosper. Fight in the cause of Allah those who fight you, but do not transgress limits; for Allah does not love transgressors. And slay them wherever you catch them, and turn them out from where they have turned you out; for tumult and oppression are worse than slaughter; but do not fight them at the Sacred Mosque, unless they first fight you there; but if they fight you, slay them. Such is the reward of those who suppress faith. But if they cease, Allah is Oft-forgiving, Most Merciful. And fight them on until there is no more tumult or oppression, and there prevail justice and faith in Allah; but if they cease, let there be no hostility except to those who practice oppression. The prohibited month for the prohibited month – and so for all things prohibited – there is the law of equality. If then any one transgresses the prohibition against you, transgress you likewise against him: But fear Allah, and know that Allah is with those who restrain themselves. And spend of your sustenance in the cause of Allah, and do not make your own hands contribute to your destruction; but do good; for Allah loves those who do good." (2:189-195)

A close analysis of the above verses will reveal to us that killing is enjoined in the form of command by Allah, 'fight'; and no one but Allah may issue such a command; it is not the kind of command that the *taghoots* of the earth will issue to their soldiers to fight: it is here a specified act. It is Allah who is commanding – a *taghoot* is not justified in commanding the slaying of people.
The act of fighting is a cause-linked matter; it is embarked on 'in the cause of Allah' – it is not in self defense, as may be attested in the behavior of Adam's better son; nor is it embarked on in defense of the home country, as the prophets abandoned their homelands and emigrated. The only cause one may fight for is 'in the cause of Allah': that about the target.
As for who we may fight, that again has been specified by Allah the Almighty in a conditional structure: 'if they fight you, slay them.' It is clear enough: killing may take place only against

a person or persons who aggress against us, 'the aggressor'. Allah calls the one who starts the fighting as a transgressor, and asserts that he does not love the transgressors. It is a decisive difference between the upright and the transgressor, that the former will not be the first to attack, and the latter will be the first to attack. You may see in a simple calculation of the above verses how many times the other's aggressive act is stipulated as a prior condition for fighting him:

Fight in the cause of Allah ° those who fight you
turn them out from where ° they have turned you out
but do not fight them at the Sacred Mosque, ° unless they first fight you there
but if they fight you, ° slay them
but if they cease, ° let there be no hostility

This conditional structure must be a fighter's chart, by which he may be guided in determining his aim and shooting in the right direction, and in determining the starting point. A pious person will not be the first to start fighting, even when it is in the cause of Allah, for a God-fearing person realizes the many restrictions which he must take count of in his life.

Once an aggressor has ceased to aggress, the license a God-fearing person had been given is nil and expired: killing is not in revenge on the enemy; and therefore, once they have ceased to fight, a pious person is commanded to hold off and cease, in obedience to Allah's commands.

In the same way as Allah specifies those whom we fight are, He specifies who we, the fighters, are: We are the God-fearing: Just before 'fight' in the verses above, we have 'fear Allah.' To apply all ten terms of God-fearing, and to be observe them all, is a basic condition that must be met before one engages in fighting: it is the God-fearing who are addressed with the command of fighting.

Hence, the word 'you' whenever it occurs in the above verses, refers to the pious, the God-fearing. So who are the God-fearing?

There are ten things specified by Allah, which, if observed by a person, then he is among the God-fearing. The ten terms have been stated together in the Qur'an:

"Say: Come, I will rehearse what Allah has really prohibited you from .. that you may be pious." (6:151-153). About these ten terms, one may refer to the chapter we have devoted to describing the God-fearing.

Allah also specifies how intensively we are to fight:

"If then any one transgresses the prohibition against you, transgress you likewise against him." (2:194)

It is in order to mention here that before embarking on fighting, a pious person must fulfill the traits of piety and its fundamentals, first of which being that he wards injury with good deeds; he is the type of man who, if someone strikes him on the right cheek, will turn to him the other also. But when you see him engaged in fighting you will know him for what he is: whether he is a wretched weakling, or a resolute and robust person. That is why you hear some simple-minded ignorant people wonder how can you intimidate someone who comes on his own to blast himself next to you?

That shows how ignorant the West is about religion: it takes it be weak, exploited by the *taghoots*, as long as it does not fight them. Not fighting a *taghoot* is taken to be a sign of weakness and defeatism. That is why I said at the beginning of this book that the White House and its Arab and non-Arab counselors have no idea what they are dealing with.

It also transpires that the degree of retaliation must be just equal to the transgression: a God-fearing believer may not retaliate with more intensity than the provoking aggression, for killing and aggression are not an endowment, nor are they a medal displayed on heroes' chests – it is indeed a heavy burden, a demanding responsibility which is embarked on to ward off danger from the Kingdom which has been established on a foundation of jihad and not fighting.

2. When Is Fighting Prohibited to a God-fearing Believer?

We recite the words of the Almighty Lord in the Qur'an:

"Allah does not forbid you, with regard to those who do not fight you for your faith nor drive you out of your homes, from dealing kindly and justly with them: for Allah loves those who are just. Allah only forbids you, with regard to those who fight you for your faith, and drive you out of your homes, and support others in driving you out, from turning to them for friendship and protection. It is such as turn to them in these circumstances that do wrong." (60:8-9)

By analyzing these verses in the same way as we did with the previous ones, we find that Allah is pointing out two classes of people: one to be treated kindly, and that is those who have not fought us for our faith (that is those who do not use weapons against us merely for our saying: Allah is my Lord;) such people Allah commands us to be kind and just to them.

The other group of people we have been commanded to keep aloof from them, and not to be friends with them: they are those who fight us for our religion and turn us out of our homes. Allah then warns those who fail to obey Him, i.e. by mixing freely with the last group as being wrong doers. Wrong doers have been described in another verse of the Qur'an as unbelievers. About this second group we are commanded by Allah to fight if they initiate fighting, and never to take for allies.

We may say, then, that man is subject to restrictions, at the beginning of the road, and at the destination; about those he is to befriend during his progress, and whom to avoid. Allah has willed that we come into contact with two groups of people on our way:

1. A group we shall have to combat and to fight: it is those who choose to start fighting against us. But Allah determines about our fighting that it must be of the same intensity as theirs, not less and not more.
2. A group we have been commanded by Allah to deal with in kindness and justice – that is the group who do not fight us, who adhere to peace, neither transgressing, nor initiating fighting. About such people the Almighty says:

"So, if they hold aloof from you and wage not war against you and offer you peace, Allah allows you no way against them." (4:90) Elsewhere He says:

"But if the enemy incline toward peace, you also incline toward peace, and trust in Allah: for He is the One that hears and knows all things." (8:61)

The verses discussing fighting in the Qur'an are many: they specify the techniques of fighting, its nature and its conditions; but the Muslim has lost his way, and the problem is compounded by his being ignorant that he has lost his way – since he does not refer to the conditions and restrictions laid down by Allah. There is not a ray of guidance in the Muslims' way so far: our hope is in their trying to conceive the definitions I put forth in the present work and in the previous one (*Ignorance and Violence*); I mean my attempt at specifying the exact meanings of such common words as: the Muslim, the believer, the pious, the unbeliever, the unjust, the miscreant, the trespasser, the sinful, and so forth; not only to conceive the right denotation and connotation of words but to realize them in one's life; for a righteous believer will listen attentively to utterances and then work upon the best of what he has heard: that is the real condition of good guidance, and no guidance is possible without realizing that condition.

Such definitions, drawn from Allah's Scripture, together with Allah's law in the world, are the alphabet of Allah's religion – no proper comprehension is possible without that alphabet. Such definitions exist in my books, but one may find them directly in the Qur'an. What I do is just to point out those definitions.

Now the pivotal point about fighting is that it is to be done for the protection of the fundamentals of Allah's Kingdom. That such Kingdom does not exist at present has led to four evils:

1. Tyranny,
2. Trespassing,
3. Oppression, and
4. Mischief.

It is on account of that that you find globalization run in the world by the earth's *taghoots*. Since globalization, in its current form, professes trespassing: It spreads mischief. Think about Christ's saying:

"By their fruit you will recognize them." (Matthew, 7:16)

The rule about the concept of jihad is that it is called for before Allah's Kingdom is established, while fighting is called for if the conditions for it are fulfilled. That will be for protecting Allah's Kingdom, only if it had been brought into being through jihad, and not through fighting: it is the *taghoot* who establishes his kingdom through fighting and coercion. Allah's messengers, on the other hand, did not resort to fighting or coercion for building the Kingdom – hence Christ's saying:

"Resist not evil." (Matthew, 5:39) And his saying: "All that take the sword shall perish with the sword." (Matthew, 26:52) That goes for all messengers of Allah, for, as we find in the Qur'an:
"For no change will you find in Allah's way of dealing: no turning off will you find in Allah's way of dealing." (35:43)

One application of this we may find in a detail of the Prophet's life: The companions of the Prophet told him, "In jahiliyah 'i.e. pre-Islam period', people used to hold us in awe, O Messenger of Allah." And he used to say to one of the oppressed families, "Be patient, O family of Yaser; it is in Paradise that we shall be together." That was so until Allah's Kingdom was established. Then, Allah revealed His timely sanction:

"To those against whom war is made, permission is given to fight, because they are wronged – and verily, Allah is Most Powerful for their aid." (22:39)

As for when to fight, it is determined in the verses next to the one just quoted:

"They are those who have been expelled from their homes in defiance of right – for no cause except that they say, 'Our Lord is Allah.' Did not Allah check one set of people by means of another, there would surely have been pulled down monasteries, churches, synagogues, and mosques, in which the name of Allah is commemorated in abundant measure. Allah will certainly aid those who aid His cause – for verily Allah is Full of strength, Exalted in might, able to enforce His will. They are those who, if We establish them in the land, establish regular prayer and give regular charity, enjoin the right and forbid wrong: with Allah rest the end and decision of all affairs." (22:40-41)

And, for a generalization, we may look at the following verse,

"Whatever beings there are in heavens and the earth do prostrate themselves to Allah acknowledging subjection – with good-will or in spite of themselves: so do their shadows in the mornings and evenings." (13:15)

According to which prostration to Allah is to be by good-will, through following in the steps of prophets: their way was to adopt the principle of: " No compulsion in religion: truth stands our clear from error: whoever rejects evil and believes in Allah has grasped to the most trustworthy hand-hold, that never breaks. And Allah hears and knows all things. Allah is the Protector of those who have faith: from the depths of darkness He will lead them forth into light." (the Qur'an, 2:256-257)

While, by the same verse, if you prostrate 'in spite of yourself', it comes by through the *taghoots* of the earth having dominance over you: for they attain rule through compulsion and terrorist means (though they would call it a revolution or a coup d'état;) and that is what is called 'by compulsion'. To distinguish the one from the other, you need to look at their fruit, at the outcome of their effort: you may look at man in the earth when he is hungry, naked, slain, hacked, chased, stripped of his rights; when Gaddafi pays two million dollars per person in blood money; and when a slain person in Afghanistan or Iraq is worth twenty dollars, which may or may not be paid; and when in Palestine, Rwanda, Bosnia, or Chechen man is slain for nothing! So I leave the verdict to the reader, for he or she can see and hear.

The other point about the concept of fighting, that it is forbidden before the Kingdom is established, while it is personally enjoined on a believer when its time comes, we may find support in the Almighty's saying,

"To those against whom war is made, permission is given to fight, because they are wronged – and verily, Allah is Most Powerful for their aid. They are those who have been expelled from their homes in defiance of right – for no cause except that they say, 'Our Lord is Allah.' " (22:39-40)

Let's reflect on the expression 'permission is given' in the above verses. It describes a believer who had been fought against, rather than being himself the fighting party; he had been expelled from his home, without resistance on his part; he had been peaceful, patient, submitting to the Lord, observant of what Allah had revealed: such was the person on whom fighting was forced, in spite of himself. Reflect also on another verse of the Qur'an:

"Fighting is prescribed for you, and you dislike it. But it is possible that you dislike a thing which is good for you, and that you love a thing which is bad for you. But Allah knows, and you know not." (2:216)

Let's look again at the previous verses, at the verse,

"They are those who, if We establish them in the land, establish regular prayer and give regular charity, enjoin the right and forbid wrong: with Allah rest the end and decision of all affairs." (22:41)

We see here a group who hold to the fundamentals of Islam, holding back from indecent deeds; from sins and trespassing, from assigning partners to Allah, or claiming false things about Allah.

It is interesting to note here the expression 'if We establish them in the land': that type of believer does not occupy lands, nor does he extort them from their rightful owners.

Allah does mention in another context that killing can take place by mistake, but even then, the perpetrator is ordained to compensate for his deed. It will be noted how, even when it is done by mistake, killing is sternly treated – and that is so to illustrate how grave the act of killing must be regarded; it may not go without compensation. So let's read the relevant verses in the Qur'an:

"Never should a believer kill a believer; but if it so happens by mistake, compensation is due: if one so kills a believer, it is ordained that he should free a believing slave, and pay compensation to the deceased's family, unless they remit it freely. If the deceased belonged to a people at war with you, and he was a believer, the freeing of a believing slave is enough. If he belonged to a people with whom you have a treaty of mutual alliance, compensation should be paid to his family, and a believing slave be freed. For those who find this beyond their means, is prescribed a fast of two months running; by way of repentance to Allah: for Allah has all knowledge and all wisdom. If a man kills a believer intentionally, his recompense is Hell, to abide therein for ever: and the wrath and the curse of Allah are upon him, and a dreadful penalty is prepared for him." (4:92-93)

It may be further noted in the above verses how the penitent acts on the part of the perpetrator are constructive contributions to society: freeing a slave, paying blood money, or fasting: in all cases, the individual is made to realize the enormity of his deed. That about killing by mistake: as for intentional killing, its penalty is Hell, wherein a perpetrator is destined to dwell for ever, with Allah's wrath and curse upon him, and a dreadful penalty is prepared for him (the Qura'n, 4:93). Let's analyze the verse more graphically: If a man kills a believer intentionally:

his recompense is Hell, to abide therein for ever ○ the wrath of Allah is upon him ○ the curse of Allah is upon him ○ a dreadful penalty is prepared for him.

Immediately next to the above verses we have:

"O you who believe! When you go abroad in the cause of Allah, investigate carefully, and do not say to any one who offers you a salutation: 'You are not a believer.' " (4:94)

Can you find anywhere a more expressive representation of the acts of killing that takes place nowadays? Muslims direct their faces toward the Qibla (in Mecca) five times a day, and they say in the course of their prayer, addressing the Lord:
"Show us the straight way, the way of those on whom You have bestowed Your grace, those whose portion is not wrath, and who do not go astray." (the Qur'an, 1:6-7)

Now that straight way is demonstrated in the Holy Qur'an itself, in ten terms, as we mentioned above, in Chapter 6, verses (151-153). But Muslims do not look at this: they go to *taghoot*-controlled scholars, who will issue them a fatwa condoning killing or sanctioning the Iraqi election. Can there be a more heart-rending tragedy!

When Isaiah was sent to the children of Israel, and he observed how they lived, he said, as is recorded in the Bible:
"The ox knoweth his owner, and the ass his master's crib: but Israel doth not know, my people doth not consider." (Isaiah, 1:3)

Let me conclude with saying that so many catch words are flying in the air, and it is very likely that they may submerge more worthy concepts. So if the reasonable individual cannot reflect on where things are drifting, if he is unable to consider where we are heading: if the thinking believers are made insensible under the pressure of the daily agonies of the *ummah* (the Muslim nation), as it has endured for long ages – then the horizon of the future appears grim, with all the treacherous efforts, which are around us on all sides. It is such reality that enjoins on us to take the responsibility of investigation and realistic analysis: only that can help us encounter the gloomy realities surrounding us in this global village; especially are responsible those who claim to have patience and dedication.

It is for such considerations that I undertake here to shed some light, and to carefully analyze the many problems related to jihad on the one hand, and to fighting on the other.

CHAPTER ELEVEN

Men

As we said above, the Qur'an is comprised of five intertwining and overlapping topics – religion being a composite of all five topics: the five topics are:

- Allah
- Man
- Allah's laws
- Allah's Scriptures
- Allah's creation

I'll be taking each of these topics in detail, but I'll devote special attention to man, to Allah, to Allah's laws, and to the relationships among these three topics, the complex network among them. I'll elaborate on the relationship between these topics: Man's relationship with Allah, man's relationship with the universe, the relationship between the Scriptures and the universe, between Allah and the universe. I'll inquire: What are the Scriptures? What is Allah? What is man? That will help us comprehend the reality of religion, the overall network, and the interrelations among its constituents: the purpose of course it to dispel the vagueness that enwraps religion, its function, and its most vital features.

1. Man

The concept of man in the Qur'an is tackled from several angles: First, Allah introduces to us the situation before man's creation; then Allah describes what man is; next, He explains the characteristics of man's relationship with Allah, with His religion, with the Hereafter, and man's relationship with prophets.

As we said above, Allah chose man, even before he was created, to undertake the development of the planet on which he would live, as we may read about that in the following verse from the Qur'an:

"Behold, your Lord said to the angels: 'I will create a vicegerent o earth.' They said: 'Will you place therein one who will make mischief therein and shed blood? – while we do celebrate Your praises and glorify Your holy name?' He said: 'I know what you do not know.'" (2: 30)

While the mountains shrank from bearing the trust, man accepted to bear it (See the Qur'an, 33: 72). But man was subjugated to crushing tyranny; and he sank into debilitating despair which took hold as a result of the absence of dignity, opportunities of honorable life, employment, and reasonable prosperity; and as a result of the monopolized authority, the concentration of wealth in the hands of a minority, the rigid division into classes; and all the other aspects of the bleak scene of life on this small planet: man has invariably lived in this quagmire. But let it be said here that all the above are not the disease, but symptoms of the disease. Once you specify the disease of our sick man and administer the right medication, you will see how the symptoms disappear, and this sick man in the earth will be himself, and will be fit for the trust he had born for too long; how he will cease to be unjust and ignorant of his part.

Man lost his way when he was deluded by the flag, a mere rag of cloth: he forgot that his allegiance was to be to his Creator, and not to a rag that fluttered at the top of a post. Man has failed to conceive the origin of that trust he has been entrusted with, and so he has been forlorn, bent down with his despair, in a way that it is true of him what the following words of Allah say:

"Allah set forth another parable of two men: one of them dumb, with no power of any sort; a wearisome burden is he to his master; whichever way he directs him, he brings no good: is such a man equal with one who commands justice, and is on a straight way? To Allah belongs the mystery of the heavens and the earth." (16: 76-77)

For man to be able to fulfill his duty, and to attain the target set for him, the objective of his placement on this planet; for man to be efficient, patient and perseverant – he needs to break free from his complexes: for today's Muslim is truly handicapped by the spiritual paralysis on the one hand, and the moral on the other. He is repressed by a paranoid apprehension that has no justification in the real world. Our first task is freeing man, spiritually and morally, for man's potentials remain inactive through his enslavement to the earth's *taghoots*, on the one hand; and, on the other, the burden of false restrictions and inherited culture embodied in the cleric, in a way that man is paralyzed by this opium, though he was meant by Allah to be an honored being.

Well did Christ realize this condition to which man descended, and in words that are the cure for this disease he said to the clergymen:

"O generation of vipers, how can ye, being evil, speak good things?" (Matthew, 12:34)

He well realized the corruption in the clergy; and he realized too the injustice of the earth's *taghoots* and business people, as may be attested by his saying:

"Ye know that the princes of the Gentiles exercise dominion over them, and they that are great exercise authority upon them. But it shall not be so among you: but whosoever will be great among you, let him be your minister; and whosoever will be chief among you, let him be your servant: Even as the Son of Man came not to be ministered unto, but to minister, and to give his life a ransom for many." (Matthew, 20: 25-28)

And so the nucleus (man) may well be crippled by the obstacles of dreading the local authorities, which really work in unison with the earth's *taghoots*; and when this happens you find man quite at a loss as to the way he may make some changes in the situation around him. The way out of course is to rid man of the obstacles that waste his powers, in order to be enabled, morally and as a human, to raise his output to a level of efficiency. Now when you think about that, you will realize that there is only one way for man: that he focuses his attention on building his spiritual power, his communion with and allegiance to his Creator, to get beyond that unjustified complex, which is enhanced by the deluding clerics, who have come to be an obstacle in the way of people – for they neither pass through the gate of salvation, nor would they let others pass and get over their wretched state. Breaking free from the *taghoot*-controlled priests on the one hand, and the *taghoot* himself on the other, is now a vital necessity: it is so since real freedom is latent in man's spirit, and nowhere else; it remains repressed as a result of fear and the intellectual and moral persecution. And so, unless this intellectual persecution is uprooted, man's potentials will remain curbed and buried inside him, thwarted through this double repression under which the Muslim groans today. But where should this march towards change start?

Change must be decisive and radical, never in the form of a compromise and concessions to the *taghoot* or the priest who sits in the *taghoot's* lap; nor to that who lies in ambush intending to kill the *taghoot*. The idols of parties and nationalism must disappear, and the trumpets of authority must be avoided while pinpointing the principles of allegiance and separation at the very root of proper thought. Landmarks of detachment must be laid down, so that one is separated from those who do not submit to Allah's command, whether they happen to be members of one's own family or one's community. Man must realize, too, that the *taghoot* and the imam both call to unity, while Allah calls to separation and detachment.

That is essential for full development of the nucleus (man), for Allah's law to quite settle in his spirit; and for His commandments and pillars to take root in the depths of the mind; for the spirit's direct communion with the Creator; and for the nucleus's realization of what the Creator wills and what He does not will, what He likes and what He dislikes; so that the extent of the nucleus's knowledge keeps expanding, and so does widen the circle of his obedience, dedication and devotion to the Creator. Once this is realized the politician or the *taghoot*-controlled clerics will not be able to deflect the nucleus or misrepresent the pillars of religion.

When the Almighty Creator describes the stages of man's delusion and guidance, He identifies about forty stages; and we shall go through some of these below, so that the nucleus has a clear idea about those stages.

What Are Man's Traits?
Referring to the Qur'an, we find that Allah describes people's traits in many verses. Some are the following:

- "Can he who was dead, to whom We gave life, and a light whereby he can walk amongst men, be like him who is in the depths of darkness, from which he can never come out? Thus to those without faith their deeds seem pleasing." (6: 122)

- "Of the people there are some who say: 'We believe in Allah and the Last Day'; but they do not really believe. Fain would they deceive Allah and those who believe, but they only deceive themselves, and realize it not! In their hearts is a disease; and Allah has increased their disease: and grievous is the penalty they incur, because they are false to themselves. When it is said to them: 'Do not make mischief on the earth,' they say: 'Why, we only want to make peace! Of a surety, they are the ones who make mischief, but they do not realize it." (2: 8-12)

- "And there is the type of man who gives his life to earn the pleasure of Allah; and Allah is full of kindness to His devotees." (2: 207)

- "There are men who say: 'Our Lord! Give us Your bounties in this world!' But they will have no portion in the Hereafter." (2: 200)

- "There is the type of man whose speech about this world's life may dazzle you, and he calls Allah to witness about what is in his heart; yet he is the most contentious of enemies. When he turns his back, his aim everywhere is to spread mischief through the earth and destroy crops and cattle. But Allah does not love mischief. When it is said to him, 'Fear Allah,' he is led by arrogance to more crime. Enough for him is Hell – an evil bed indeed to lie on!" (2: 204-206)

- "Then there are among men such as say, 'We believe in Allah;' but when they suffer affliction in the cause of Allah they treat men's oppression as if it were the wrath of Allah! And if help comes to you from your Lord, they are sure to say, 'We have always been with you!' Does not

Allah know best all that it in the hearts of all Creation?" (29, 10)

- "But there are, among men, those who purchase idle tales, without knowledge or meaning, to mislead men from the path of Allah and throw ridicule on the path: for such there will be a humiliating penalty. When our signs are rehearsed to such a one, he turns away in arrogance, as if he did not hear them, as if there were deafness in both his ears: announce to him a grievous penalty." (31: 6-7)

- "Yet there are among men those who dispute about Allah, without knowledge and without guidance, and without a book to enlighten them! When they are told to follow the revelation that Allah has sent down, they say: 'Nay, we shall follow the ways that we found our fathers following.' What! Even if it is Satan beckoning them to the penalty of the Blazing Fire?" (31: 20-21)

- "There are among men some who serve Allah, as it were, on the verge: if good befalls them, they are, therewith, well content; but if a trial comes to them, they turn on their faces: they lose both this world and the Hereafter: that is loss for all to see! They call on such deities, besides Allah, as can neither hurt nor profit them: that is straying far indeed from the way." (22: 11-12)

Some profile may be drawn from the above verses about the kind of being man is – his relationship with his Lord, his distinguishing traits, and his destination. From the above glimpses one may glean some light to distinguish a Muslim, a believer, a pious person, a disbeliever, etc. That will provide a nucleus with the necessary tool for recognizing people on the one hand, and for taking note of their shortcomings on the other.

Relationship of Allah with man:

The relationship of Allah with man has been defined by Allah's saying in the Qur'an:

"Allah is Most Kind and Most Merciful to man." (22: 65)

It is right to start from this point and the to note how the circle gets wider, where the relationship between Allah and man goes along set courses, reaching up to certain destinations; courses which are based on Allah's discourse to man, instructing him about his origin and his destination, and teaching him the system which ensures his good and his well-being. Let's review some verses from the Qur'an that bear on this:

- "O mankind! If you have a doubt about the Resurrection, consider that We created you out of dust." (22: 5)
- "O men! Here is a parable set forth! Listen to it!" (22: 73)
- "O men! Certainly the promise of Allah is true. Let not then this present life deceive you." (35: 5)
- "O you men! It is you that have need of Allah: but Allah is the One Free of all wants, Worthy of all praise." (35: 15)
- "O mankind! We created you from a single pair of male and female, and made you into nations and tribes, that you may know one another. Verily the most honored of you in the sight of Allah is he who is the most righteous of you. And Allah has full knowledge and is well acquainted with all things." (49: 13)

The relationship between Allah and man, as represented in Allah's discourse directed to man, is given so that Allah may direct man as to his origin and destination, and to instruct him concerning the doctrine he is to follow in his life.

CHAPTER TWELVE

The God-fearing

Allah points out the conditions that indicate fearing Allah, all in one verse of the Qur'an,

"It is not righteousness that you turn your faces toward east or west; but it is righteousness – to believe in Allah and the Last Day, and the angels, and the Book, and the messengers; to spend of your substance, out of love for Him, for your kin, for the orphans, for the needy, for the wayfarer, for those who ask, and for the ransom of slaves; to be steadfast in prayer, and practice regular charity; to fulfil the contracts which you have made; and to be firm and patient, in pain and adversity and throughout all periods of panic. Such are the people of truth, those who fear Allah." (2:177)

What we have here are the conditions and levels of fearing Allah, starting with faith in Allah, and covering a whole range down to steadfastness in pain and adversity and throughout all periods of panic. Once a human has well fulfilled the above conditions he is deemed a God-fearing person

Not only does Allah specify the terms of fearing Allah, but He classifies the God-fearing into two groups:

The first group: those who believe in the Unseen, are steadfast in prayer, and spend out of what Allah has provided them, and

The second group: those who believe in the Revelation sent to the prophet, and sent before his time, and have in their hearts the assurance of the Hereafter (See the Qur'an, 2: 3-4)

You will find these two groups in existence at the time of any prophet. One example of the first group is those who believed in the Unseen, wrote down what Christ, peace be upon him, said, as prophesied in books, but did not write down what was revealed to Christ, peace be upon him or the groups before him, having descended to him from the prophets before him: teaching that had been revealed to them, and Christ inherited their books. It is for this reason that Christ said:

"All things are delivered to me of my Father."
(Matthew, 11: 27)

It is those books which were delivered to him, and which had been revealed to the prophets and messengers before him, that he had in mind when he said:

"Ye do err, not knowing the scriptures."
(Matthew, 22:29)

Every prophet or messenger prior to Christ inherited those before him. That is why you find in the Bible,

"The law and the prophets were until John."
(Luke, 16:16)

Which denotes that John, peace be upon him, was the only heir before Christ, peace be upon him: hence the latter's saying:

"And I will pray the Father, and he shall give you another Comforter, that he may abide with you for ever; even the Spirit of truth; whom the world cannot receive, because it seeth him not, neither knoweth him: but ye know him; for he dwelleth with you, and shall be in you." (Luke, 14:16-17)

'ye know him; for he dwelleth with you,' that is to say: if you look into that which is in the Qur'an, you would find it identical with that which you had been taught by Jesus, that which is in the Bible, though most people do not comprehend it.

And again, those who believed in Muhammad, peace be upon him, the same as prophesied in previous Books and the Scriptures revealed before him, must believe in the Scriptures he inherited from Christ, and which were rerevealed to Muhammad, peace be upon him, by Allah – they comprise the Qur'an, revealed in seven different styles: this much was announced by Muhammad, peace be upon him, when he said: "I have been granted the Qur'an in seven styles." Indeed, scholars have disputed long about the exact meaning of this tradition, their opinion diversifying to forty different views concerning that. (See p. 61 of *Al-Itqan fi 'ulum al-Qur'an*, by Jalalu-d-Din 'Abdul-Rahman al-Suyuti, who died in 911 A.H (1505 C.E.).; pub. Al-Ma'rifah Publishing House, Beirut, Lebanon.) See also *Ghaith al-Naf' fi al-Qira'at al-Sab'*, by Ali Nuri al-Safaqisi. In the above sources a reader finds the tradition narrated by no less than twenty five companions of the prophet, peace be upon him, including Ubay bin Ka'b, Anas, Huthayfah bin al-Yaman, Zaid bin Arqam, Samurah bin Jundub. It was declared by Abu Ubaid to be of the highest rank of authenticity, designated 'mutawater' (i.e. conveyed in so many independent ways to make it virtually impossible to be suspected of falsehood) in the terminology of specialists." In one report, mentioned by Abu Ya'la in his *Musnad*, Uthman, the third caliph, stood one day on the pulpit and commanded people: I exhort, in the Name of Allah, any man who heard the Prophet, peace and blessings of Allah be on him, say: "The Qur'an was revealed in seven styles, each fulfilling and perfect for its purpose;" that such man should stand up. And then an incalculable number of men stood, and attested to the truth of the tradition. Seeing this, Uthman said: "And I add my testimony." Here Abu Ya'la mentions the point of about forty different interpretations of the tradition. Those interested may refer to the book mentioned above.

So, we have here two groups, taking two opposite attitudes concerning time, one believing in what is to come, and the other believing in what has passed away before. Both groups affiliate to the same religion, and both merit the designation of 'pious or God-fearing' people. As for the Book or Scripture, revealed before Muhammad, and mentioned at the beginning of the second Chapter of the Qur'an as a guidance for the God-fearing, it is included entirely in that same volume, the Holy Qur'an. About that inclusion, we have more in another verse of the Qur'an:

"A messenger from Allah, rehearsing scriptures kept pure and holy: Wherein are decrees right and straight." (98: 2-3)

Indeed, the Almighty Allah has shed glaring light on the traits of the God-fearing person, every time stressing certain aspects of his. At one spot, He describes the pious as that who puts forth the truth and confirms it (the Qur'an, 39:33). Getting back to the Second Chapter, verse 177 we find that righteousness is linked to fearing Allah, although the same conditions are laid down in both locations.

To come to a precise definition of who is the God-fearing is of the utmost importance, because that is the trait which characterizes the nucleus, who bears the responsibility of erecting Allah's Kingdom. There are ten terms which must be fulfilled for one to be among the God-fearing: it is that and not what the *taghoot*-controlled scholars claim. It must be shown in practice and dedication in real-life situations. Now those ten terms are to be found in the words of Allah, the Almighty, so let's refer to the Qur'an:

"Say: 'Come, I will rehearse what Allah has prohibited you from': join not any thing as equal with Him; be good to your parents, kill not your children on a plea of want – We provide sustenance for you and for them – do not come near to shameful deeds, whether open or secret; take not life, which Allah has made sacred, except by way of justice and law: thus does He command you, that you may learn wisdom. And come not near to the orphan's property, except to improve it, until he attain the age of full strength; give measure and weight with full justice – no burden do We place on any soul, but that which it can bear – whenever you speak, speak justly even if a near relative is concerned; and fulfil the Covenant of Allah: thus He commands you, that you may remember. Verily, this is My way, leading straight: follow it: do not follow other paths: they will scatter you about from His Path: thus He commands you, that you may be God-fearing." (6: 151-153)

Let's now read the same verses, breaking them down into items:

Say: 'Come, I will rehearse what Allah has prohibited you from':

1. join not any thing as equal with Him;
2. be good to your parents,
3. kill not your children on a plea of want – We provide sustenance for you and for them –
4. do not come near to shameful deeds, whether open or secret;
5. take not life, which Allah has made sacred, except by way of justice and law: thus does He command you, that you may learn wisdom.
6. And come not near to the orphan's property, except to improve it, until he attain the age of full strength;

7. give measure and weight with full justice – no burden do We place on any soul, but that which it can bear –

8. whenever you speak, speak justly even if a near relative is concerned;

9. and fulfil the Covenant of Allah: thus He commands you, that you may remember.

10. Verily, this is My way, leading straight: follow it: do not follow other paths: they will scatter you about from His Path: thus He commands you, that you may be God-fearing.

By a close look at the above verses one can comprehend the terms of fearing Allah, all of which are confined to not taking any partner to Allah as the primary term, and to acting in line with the straight path of Allah, the way which was laid down by Him alone.

By getting on with our investigation of the Qur'an we find that Allah defines the pious further and sheds more light on their traits from a different perspective, as we find in the following verse:

"It is not righteousness that you turn your faces toward east or west; but it is righteousness – to believe in Allah and the Last Day, and the angels, and the Book, and the messengers; to spend of your substance, out of love for Him, for your kin, for orphans, for the needy, for the wayfarer, for those who ask, and for the ransom of slaves; to be steadfast in prayer, and practice regular charity; to fulfil the contracts which you have made; and to be firm and patient, in pain and adversity and throughout all periods of panic. Such are the people of truth, those who fear Allah." (2: 177)

Again, what we have in the above verse are the terms of God-fearing: they are linked to truthfulness and to doing goodness, in a full cycle. By reviewing both definitions, we may have a clear view of the terms of God-fearing which man is bound to fulfil in order to reach the state which entitles him to erect the Kingdom of Allah.

God-fearing, faith, Islam, patience, jihad, disbelief and idolatry are not mere words uttered by mouth – they actually denote matters of utmost preciseness; they indicate fine-grained terms of conditions, articles, covenants and pacts of man with his Lord. To fail to comprehend those terms fully and precisely, to fail to reconsider the definition in detail, or to probe its bases and source, man will not attain to the rank of fully conceiving the essence of religion and its invaluable treasures.

By reviewing the stages of prophets' lives we find that they exhorted their peoples to fear Allah (Arabic: *taqwa*); that is to say they urged them to adhere to the terms which Allah had described as the terms needed to be fulfilled for His Kingdom to be erected. We also note that all the prophets adhered firmly to fearing Allah, and followed the straight path. A God-fearing person is not that who submits by showing off his Islam, by practicing prayer, fasting and pilgrimage – submission is rather adhering to the ten things we enumerated above, and to the subsidiary things that branch from the above ten things. Let's refer to the words of the Almighty in the Qur'an about that:

"Verily We have directed the People of the Book before you, and you to fear Allah." (4: 131)

As you see, the command of adhering to fearing Allah was not confined to one group or one religion, but is rather a general command for all people: that is then the true religion, and it comprises all the ten commandments.

In another verse of the Qur'an, Allah says:
"O you Messengers! Enjoy all things good and pure, and work righteousness: for I am well-acquainted with all that you do. And

verily this brotherhood of yours is a single brotherhood, and I am your Lord and Cherisher: therefore fear Me and no other." (23: 51-52)

Which demonstrates that if one follows a prophet, he has followed all prophets: the message of piety is one that was conveyed by each one of the prophets, the way marked out for success through good guidance: it is so since Allah is the One Lord; Creator; Cherisher, with no partner or equal – such as party or nationality. He has sent down one religion, a religion that is based on the five pillars that we listed above, brought up to ten with their branches. By looking again into those ten pillars we find that they do not go beyond the first five. Therefore, what you hear and see in mosques and churches nowadays is a false religion, a deluded hope, sick hallucinations that avail nothing, but rather precipitate the followers to certain misguidance.

What Allah's messengers called people to was fearing their God, and that is by fulfilling the above ten pillars: the same fundamentals professed by Jesus, peace be upon him, when he urged people to keep his commandments (John, 15:10).

But his followers misinterpreted his words, reading in them something quite different from what he had said in crystal clear language. They rather behaved in the manner described in the following verse from the Qur'an:

"Their intention is to extinguish Allah's Light by blowing with their mouths: but Allah will complete the revelation of His Light, even though the unbelievers may detest it." (61: 8)

The contrast between the two attitudes is vividly described in the Qur'an; Cain's intention to kill and Abel's reply are narrated: "Said [Cain]: 'Be sure I will slay you.' 'Surely,' said [Abel,] 'Allah accepts of the sacrifice of those who are righteous.'" (5: 27)

It was so because Abel was mindful of Allah's decree: take not life, which Allah has made sacred, except by way of justice and law (see the Qur'an, 6:151), and has deemed that as one of the conditions of fulfilling fearing Allah. True to the terms of God-fearing, Abel said, as reported in the Qur'an:

"It is not for me to stretch my hand against you to slay you: for I do fear Allah, the Cherisher of the Worlds." (5: 28)

He held back from killing his brother, and he made it clear why he would not: it was because he feared Allah, Lord of the worlds – and that is to say, "I uphold the terms of fearing Allah, both as values that settled in my spirit, and as principles that I adhere to in practice."

He would not stretch his hand to slay his brother, who was about to slay him, not even in self-defense: Abel was aware that murder was not to be, even in self-defense, for God-fearing was a commandment of Allah to man, as we read elsewhere in the Qur'an:

"Help one another in righteousness and piety, but do not help one another in sin and rancor." (5:2)

So let us ask this: When Sunnis and Shiites kill each other is their behavior that of Cain or Abel?

Do they help one another in righteousness and piety, or in sin and rancor?

I leave the answer to the reader.

The high achievers do identify the meaning of sin and its way, and identify righteousness and piety and their pillars.

We learn from the Divine Writ in the Qur'an that the reward of the pious is securing Allah's friendship, for Allah announces that He is the Friend of the God-fearing, as we read in the following verse:

"It is only wrong-doers that stand as friend, one to another: but Allah is the Friend of the righteous." (45: 19)

Such relationship with the One Who Created everything in the best proportion will provide man with support in adversity, a backing that never fails, a treasure that is more precious than all the falsehood of the deceivers: He will find that support when man has to encounter the world, standing for truth, and submitting to Him Who Created all, invoking His support and keeping His guidance in view.

Only thus will man be counted among those who willingly prostrate themselves to Allah, by fulfilling the terms of that prostration.

CHAPTER THIRTEEN

The Successful

For one who seeks right guidance in the Holy Qur'an, he needs to approach it with a sound heart, lest misguidance leads him astray: that is first; and second he needs to realize that the clues to guidance are to be sought in heaven, that the Almighty has the supreme power. The prophets well understand the full meaning of God's words in the Qur'an:

"If you call them to guidance, they do not hear. You will see them looking at you, but they do not see." (7:198)

And the Almighty's saying in another verse:

"No soul can believe, except by the Will of Allah." (10:100)

As an illustration of the above you may take the words of Noah, peace be upon him, as reported in the Qur'an:

"Of no profit will be my counsel to you, much as I desire to give you good counsel, if it be that Allah wills to leave you astray." (11:34)

Such declaration on the part of Noah is based on a law of Allah's, reported in the Qur'an, where the Almighty says:

"Those who behave arrogantly on the earth in defiance of right – I will turn them from My Signs: Even if they see all the Signs they will not believe in them; and if they see the way of right conduct, they will not accept it as the Way; but if they see the way of error, that is the way they will adopt. For they have rejected Our Signs, and failed to take warning from them." (7:146)

What is required here is first a sensitivity of conscience, a transparency of spirit, a constant fear of Allah, and a continual vigilance; and second doing deeds that are a demonstration of faith. These two requirements are the corner-stone for those who seek guidance and success: As mentioned above, you cannot fill a bottle with water until you have expelled the air inside it. And man will have to encounter some test of his faith, once or twice every year.

You may attain such noble stage after you have got beyond the thorny land of desires, greed and ambitions; after you have gone beyond the calls of this earth, the groundless phobias and apprehensions of this life; after you realize that such loyalties as nation, homeland, tribe, kin, and even children, would avail you nothing, nor can they cause you any harm in themselves: all of those are completely helpless, since benefiting and injuring are really only in the hand of the One Who created the heavens and the earth. And you will have to stand before Him alone, empty-handed, bare-footed, bearing on your back what you have earned on this earth.

Blessedness is for him who has believed; who does righteous deeds, exhorts others to truth and exhorts them to endurance.

But man will be unable to do righteous deeds, to exhort truth and patience without first having established this state in his conscience and spirit: that will come about through man's communion with his Lord, in private and in public; for that will lift the curtain from his eyes. He will have vision, and his ears will be ready to hear – then will man be able to work for erecting the Kingdom of Allah on earth: not as he desires it to be, but as the Lord of the Worlds wills.

Let's quote here a relevant statement from the Preface of *Work: Ability and Will*, a book by a rightly acclaimed writer, Jawdat Sa'eed:

"No successful work can be realized without intention and the right method: not to want something really, not to have the intention and will we do not endeavor to accomplish it. And, on the other hand, not to know the way to doing something we will not succeed in doing it." (p. 9)

Such endeavor may be guided by such words of the Almighty as the following:

"Let there arise out of you a band of people inviting to all that is good, enjoining what is right, and forbidding what is wrong: they are the ones who attain success." (3: 104)

It may be noted in the above verse how Allah defines the way to success as being through doing good, enjoining what is right, and forbidding what is wrong. The latter activity works in the way yeast works in dough.

The Almighty Allah commands justice, if one happens to rule among people; and He commands doing goodness if one is not a ruler. What is wrong has been pointed out and forbidden by the Almighty; that is when he tells us that He

- Forbids us from joining any thing as equal with Him;
- Forbids sin;

- Forbids shameful deeds;
- Forbids wrongful oppression;
- Forbids men from saying concerning Allah that which they know not.

That is then the wrong that men are bound to avoid: there is no room for enslavement to any one but Allah; there is no one to hear from, to be dictated to by anyone but Allah, the Almighty: obedience and a servile attitude are due to none but Allah, the One.

About all that we may read the following verses from the Qur'an:

"Take what the Messenger assigns to you, and deny yourselves that which he withholds from you. And fear Allah; for Allah is strict in punishment. Some part is due to the indigent immigrants [from Mecca], those who were expelled from their homes and their property, while seeking grace from Allah and His Good Pleasure, and aiding Allah and His Messenger: such are indeed the sincere ones – but those who before them, had homes [in Medina] and had adopted the faith, show their affection to such as came to them for refuge, and entertain no desire in their hearts for things given to the latter, but give them preference over themselves, even though poverty was their own lot. And those saved from the covetousness of their own souls – they are the ones that achieve prosperity." (59: 7-9)

You see how glowing an image is drawn in the above verses, held up by the Lord for all coming generations, bristling with superior selflessness: such forceful texts are meant of course to establish a bond among all the followers of this religion, from the earliest to the latest. They must feel united in a bond of solidarity, harmony, love and intimate closeness; any barrier of race and class must vanish in their spirit, as long as they go under the banner of Him Who has created and given proportion and order, Who has brought out the green and luscious pasture – they move towards a bright horizon where they hope to meet with the Kind and Merciful Allah.

Such splendid representation is today an absent fact from the practice of those who claim to be devoted and obedient servants of Allah, and lead people in mosques, while they are in fact dishonest and fraudulent thieves of spirit. We may get some enlightenment from this verse of the Qur'an:

"The answer of believers, when summoned to Allah and His Messenger, in order that he may judge between them, is no other than this: they say, 'We hear and we obey': it is such as these that will attain success." (24: 51)

So look at the state of Muslims today, when they seek the judgment of the *taghoots* of the earth, and you will realize by contrast the meaning of 'the successful'. Consider it in the light of this verse from the Qur'an:

"Then those whose balance of good deeds is heavy – they will attain success." (23: 102)

Each one will have to consider the fundamentals of God-fearing and the terms of success, then turn to his deeds and see whether he is giving his allegiance to the *taghoots* of the earth. Man will be sufficient as judge on the Last Day of his deeds (and so man will have to ask his own soul, no matter how many fatwas he hears justifying his conduct.) It may be helpful to consider these verses from the Qur'an:

"When a Sura [i.e. a chapter of the Qur'an] comes down, enjoining them to believe in Allah and do jihad with His Messenger, those with wealth and influence among them ask you for exemption, and say: 'Leave us behind: we would be with those who sit at home.' They prefer to be with those who stay behind, who remain behind at home: their hearts are sealed and so they do not understand. But the Messenger, and those who believe with him, strive with their wealth and their persons: for them are all good things: and it is they who will prosper." (9:86-88)

As for those who stay behind (Arabic: *khawalif*): We have defined above a Muslim, a person who submits to the commands of Allah and His Messenger. We have also defined a believer, a person who entertains no love for those who struggle against Allah. And we defined a *mujahed*, a person performing jihad: a *mujahed* is one who does goodness, enjoins what is good and forbids what is bad; in other words, he is a person who strives to erect the Kingdom of Allah. Mention has also been made of the patient, and that is a person who will not stop at doing what is personally enjoined on him to do: he is anxious to do his share of what is collectively enjoined on believers; and so he goes beyond the strictly personal duties and contributes some good deeds. As for the sit-still among believers, they are in two types: one type is patient, but stop at the personally enjoined duty without any genuine justification, in the form of a physical handicap or disease, or a material or physical incapacity. Another type of a sit-still person is one who is patient, but has a physical or material incapacity. And now we need to look at a third type of sit-still persons, the staying behind (*khalwalif* in Arabic): those who decline to go forth, neither doing what is personally enjoined on each believer, nor what is collectively enjoined: hence Allah calls them the stay-behind, whose hearts are sealed; He deemed them as unclean (the Qur'an, 9:95), and branded them as not apprehending (9:87), and as not of those who believe.

They should be viewed within the general rule, expressed in another location of the Qur'an:

"The balance that day [the Last Day] will be true (to a nicety): those whose scale of good will be heavy, will be successful." (7:8)

And truth, as pointed out above, is that which was put forth on the tongue of prophets; it is the balance by which things are to be weighed – it is definitely not that taught in mosques and churches.

What the unlettered prophet, Muhammad promulgated comprises the teachings of previous messengers. Let's refer to the Qur'an about that:

"He [Allah] said: 'With My punishment I visit whom I will; but My mercy extends to all things. That (mercy) I shall ordain for those who do right, and practice regular charity, and those who believe in Our signs; those who follow the Messenger, the unlettered Prophet, whom they find mentioned in their own Scriptures – in the Law and the Gospel – for he commands them as lawful what is good and pure and prohibits them from what is bad and impure; he releases them from their heavy burdens and from the yokes that are upon them. So it is those who believe in him, honor him, help him, and follow the Light which is sent down with him – it is they who will be successful." (7:156-157)

And yet people hold, unfortunately, to the myth of multiplicity of religions. But I urge the reader to go directly to the words of the Almighty, for that will undeceive him. Let him read about the pious, some of whom had lived in the past and some came later: and let him note how the book sent to all the pious, the God-fearing is a single Book. Be mindful of that when you hear what the *taghoot*-controlled scholars declare, while still in the *taghoot*'s lap. Here are some verses from the Qur'an in which is light enough:

"Alif. Lam. Mim. This is the Book: in it is guidance sure, without doubt, to those who fear Allah. Who believe in the Unseen, are steadfast in prayer, and spend out of what We have provided for them. And those who believe in the Revelation sent to you, and sent before your time, and in their hearts have the assurance of the Hereafter. They are on true guidance, from their Lord, and it is these who are the successful." (2:1-5)

And somewhere else: "Your riches and your children may be but a trial: but in the presence of Allah is the highest reward. So fear Allah as much as you can; listen and obey and spend charity for the benefit of your own souls. And those saved from the covetousness of their own souls – they are the successful ones." (64: 15-16)

Let's also recite this: "You will not find any people who believe in Allah and the Last Day, loving those who resist Allah and His Messenger, even though they were their fathers or their sons, or their brothers, or their kindred. For such He has written faith in their hearts, and strengthened them with a spirit from Himself. And He will admit them to the Gardens beneath which rivers flow, to dwell therein for ever. Allah will be well pleased with them, and they with Him. They are the Party of Allah. Truly it is the Party of Allah that will achieve success." (58:22)

Another verse says: "So give what is due to kindred, the needy, and the wayfarer. That is best for those who seek the Countenance of Allah, and it is they who will be successful." (30:38)

A last one to quote is this: "But any that in this life has repented, believed, and worked righteousness, will have hopes to be among those who achieve success." (28:67)

From the above we may draw some conclusions concerning the way to success:

- Piety is a way to success
- Performing jihad is a way to success
- Worshipping Allah and doing righteousness is a way to success
- Repentance is a way to success
- To remember Allah and to seek His blessings is a way to success
- To remember the bounty of Allah is a way to success.

And in the same way as Allah specifies who is a successful man, and specifies the way to success, he specifies those who will not prosper. Let's look at the Qur'an again:

- "Verily the wrong-doers will not prosper." (6:21)
- "Never will prosper those who sin." (10:17)
- [reporting Moses as saying] "Sorcerers will not prosper." (10:77)
- "Verily the unbelievers will fail to win through." (23:117)
- "Those who ascribe false things to Allah will never prosper." (16:116)
- "And he fails that corrupts it [his soul]." (91:10)
- "Frustration was the lot of every powerful obstinate transgressor." (14:15)
- "Hopeless indeed will be the man that carries iniquity (on his back)." (20:111)

So we do have the graded ascent to success, and the question is: when we have that does it make it easier for us to proceed towards the light of which Allah tells us ... can we go forth to join the band of the successful, as the terms of success are known to us ...?

CHAPTER FOURTEEN

The Righteous

Religion for society has the function of immunity for the body – once it is corrupted, society will be corrupted. The reality of religion has never been a means to attaining authority; so when religious parties are used as a means to getting authority, that involves a corruption of religion; it is furthermore a misrepresentation of true religion. For the reality of religion, as said above, is that it is the immunity system of society – when, for instance, you see the Muslim society so divided, corrupt and retarded, it reflects deficiency in religious thought.

So, to start this discussion, it may be said that it is for Allah, and no one else, to determine who is righteous and who is a mischief-doer. About that we read in the Qur'an:

"Allah knows the man who means mischief from the man who means good." (2:220)

Bearing this in mind, we may go to the Almighty to describe to us some of those who are righteous, and we find the following:

"Abraham was indeed a model, devoutly obedient to Allah, and true in faith, and he did not join gods with Allah. He showed his gratitude for the favors of Allah, Who chose him, and guided him to a straight way. And We gave him good in this world, and he will be, in the Hereafter, in the ranks of the righteous. So we have taught you the inspired message, follow the ways of Abraham, the true in faith, and he did not join gods with Allah." (16;120-123)

Other messengers and prophets are also enumerated by Allah, and described as righteous. Let's read more:

"And Zakariya and John, and Jesus and Elias all in the ranks of the righteous: And Isamil and Elisha. And Jonas, and Lot, etc." (6:85-90)

Turning to the Bible, we may note how Jesus, peace be upon him, declined to accept people's calling him as righteous. Let's read:

"I can of mine own self do nothing: as I hear, I judge: and my judgment is but the will of the Father which hath sent me. If I bear witness of myself, my witness is not true. There is another that beareth witness of me; and I know that the witness which he witnesseth of me is true. Ye sent unto John, and he bare witness unto the truth. But I receive not testimony from man: but these things I say, that ye might be saved." (John, 5:30-34)

And he continues to say:
"Search the scriptures; for in them ye think ye have eternal life: and they are they which testify of me. And ye will not come to me, that ye might have life. I receive not honour from men." (Ibid, 5:39-41)

Now after the above statements, a certain man came forward and asked Jesus, peace be upon him:

"Good Maser, what good thing shall I do, that I may have eternal life." And Jesus answered him,

"Why callest thou me good? there is none good but one, that is, God: but if thou wilt enter into life, keep the commandments. He saith unto him, Which? Jesus said, Thou shalt do no murder, Thou shalt not commit adultery, Thou shalt not steal Thou shalt not bear false witness. Honour thy father and thy mother: and, Thou shalt love thy neighbour as thyself. Etc." (Matthew, 19:16-19)

Now, if you were to compare what Jesus is saying here to the man with the conditions of piety in the Qur'an (6:151-153), you would find them the same.

The Almighty Lord lays down the conditions of righteousness in various verses of the Qur'an; in one location He says:

"All who obey Allah and the Messenger are in the company of those on whom is the Grace of Allah – of the prophets who teach, the sincere, the witnesses, the righteous: ah! What a beautiful fellowship! Such is the bounty from Allah: and sufficient is it that Allah knows all." (4:69-70)

He elaborates more elsewhere, where He says:

"Not all of them are alike. Of the People of the Book are a portion that stand (for the right); they rehearse the signs of Allah all night long, and they prostrate themselves in adoration. They believe in Allah and the Last Day; they enjoin what is right, and forbid what is wrong; and they hasten in emulation in all good works: they are in the ranks of the righteous. Of the good they do, nothing will be rejected of them; for Allah knows well those that do right." (3:113-115)

We find more in the Qur'an about that:
"We have enjoined on man kindness to parents: but if they (either of them) strive (to force) you to join with Me (in worship) anything of which you have no knowledge, do not obey them.

You have all to return to Me, and I will tell you the truth of all that you did. And those who believe and work righteous deeds – them We shall admit to the company of the righteous." (29:8-9)

We may find an elaborate description of what righteous deeds are in the Qur'an, so let's look at that:

"To the Madyan people We sent Shu'aib, one of their brethren: he said: 'O my people! Worship Allah: you have no other god but Him. And do not give short measure or weight: I see you in prosperity, but I fear for you the penalty of a Day that will compass you all round. And O my people! Give just measure and weight, nor withhold from the people the things that are their due: do not commit evil in the land with intent to do mischief. That which is left you by Allah is best for you, if you but believed! But I am not set over you to keep watch!' They said: 'O Shu'aiab! Does your religion of prayer command you that we leave off the worship which our fathers practiced or that we leave off doing what we like with our property? Truly, you are the one that forbears with faults and is right-minded.' He said: 'O my people! Do you see whether I have a clear sign from my Lord, and He has given me sustenance pure and good as from Himself? I do not wish, in opposition to you, to do that which I forbid you to do. I only desire your betterment to the best of my power; and my success in my task can only come from Allah. In Him I trust and to Him I look." (11:84-88)

It will be noticed that the above debate between Shu'aib and his people comprises a definition of righteousness, which is displayed in specific aspects:

1. One aspect concerns man's relation with Allah (Worship Allah: you have no other god but Him)
2. Another aspect concerns man's relation with man

3. A third concerns man's relation to the environment in which he happens to live.

The portion of Sha'aib's debate: 'do not give short measure or weight ...do not commit evil in the land with intent to do mischief,' alerts people to:

Measure .... man's relation with man

Weight: .... man's relation with the environment.

It has been Allah's will that man should have a will; it has been His will, too, that guidance should be a fruit of positive responding to this religion. It is not by the mere conveying of religion to people or expounding it: it is realized when people take it as the ultimate concern of their life, the pivot round which their life, their ambitions, and dreams revolve.

Man has been enabled to do what he wants to do: what he does is either righteous deeds or evil – there is no third alternative. What this means is that Allah divides people in accordance with the outcome of their effort, and their allegiance to their Creator. The two groups are not deemed equal in Allah's sight: and that is what Allah tells us in the Qur'an:

- "Not equal are the blind and those who see: nor are equal those who believe and work deeds of righteousness, and those who do evil." (40:58)
- "Shall We treat those who believe and work deeds of righteousness, the same as those who do mischief on earth? Shall We treat those who guard against evil, the same as those who turn aside from the right?" (38:28)
- "Allah has indeed sent down to you a Message – a messenger, who rehearses to you the Signs of Allah containing clear explanations, that he may lead forth

those who believe and do righteous deeds from the depths of darkness into light." (65:10-11)

- "Those who believe, and work righteousness – their Lord will guide them because of their faith." (10:9)

Allah also tells us the outcome of righteousness, as we may see in the following verses:

- "Before this We wrote in the Psalms, after the Message (given to Moses): 'My servants, the righteous, shall inherit the earth.' Verily in this Qur'an is a Message for people who would truly worship Allah. Verily in this is a message for people who would truly worship Allah. We sent you not, but as a mercy for all creatures." (21:105-106)

Which implies that if you do not see mercy's effects among people, you may infer that those who profess to uphold religion are really clinging to a false religion, not the one revealed by Allah.

- "Allah has promised, to those among you who believe and work righteous deeds, that He will, of a surety, grant them in the land, inheritance of power, as He granted it to those before them; that He will establish in authority their religion – the one which He has chosen for them; and that He will change their state, after the fear in which they lived, to one of security and peace: They will worship Me alone and not associate anything with Me. If any do reject faith after this, they are rebellious and wicked." (24:55)

And this means that if Allah does not grant us the inheritance of the land – if we see the *taghoots* of the earth dominate and sow evil in the earth, then mercy is absent in the earth, the entire earth. So contemplate for yourself, reflect on this and draw your own conclusions. See what is actually taking place on the earth, the entire earth, and review the definition of the rebellious in the above verse.

It will transpire that the inheritance of the earth will come by through working deeds of goodness, and not through the slaying of people, nor through allying with the *taghoots* of the earth, nor through praying behind the imams of mischief in the earth. About that we have the following in the Qur'an:

- "But he who works deeds of righteousness, and has faith, will have no fear of harm nor of any curtailment of what is his due." (20:112)
- "But such as come to Him as believers who have worked righteous deeds – for them are ranks exalted." (20:75)

If someone craves communion with the prophets in the Hereafter, and a life of dignity in this world, the way to that is to do good deeds, in the same way as the prophets did. He has to take them for model, to seek guidance in them, and not in the *taghoots* of the earth, nor in the imams of disbelief. It is absolutely essential that one perceives the type of man who is represented in the following verses of the Qur'an:

"Of the people there are some who say: 'We believe in Allah and the Last Day;' but they do not (really) believe. Fain would they deceive Allah and those who believe, but they only deceive themselves, and realize (it) not! In their hearts is a disease; and Allah has increased their disease: And grievous is the penalty they (incur), because they are false (to themselves). When it is said to them: 'Make not mischief on the earth,' they say: 'Why, we only want to make peace!' Of a surety, they are the ones who make mischief, but they realize (it) not. When it is said to them: 'Believe as the others believe;' they say: 'Shall we believe as the fools believe?' Nay, of a surety they are the fools, but they do not know. When they meet those who believe, they say: 'We believe;'

but when they are alone with their evil ones, they say: 'We are really with you: We (were) only jesting.' Allah will throw back their mockery on them, and give them rope in their trespasses; so they will wander like blind ones (to and fro). These are they who have bartered Guidance for error: But their traffic is profitless, and they have lost true direction. Their similitude is that of a man who kindled a fire; when it lighted all around him, Allah took away their light and left them in utter darkness. So they could not see. Deaf, dumb, and blind, they will not return (to the path). " (2:8-18)

CHAPTER FIFTEEN

The Unbelievers

It is in vain that, seeking to escape from the present maze, you blunder into some ancient wilderness. Sit aside for quite a while, and have communion with your self; give yourself to some inner debate; try to dig deep for your real problem: why are you there; and who is entitled to have your allegiance? The Qur'an teaches us:

"And also in your own selves: will you not then see?" (51:21)

To be in communion with your Creator, listen attentively to His Words; weigh yourself against His Straight Way: study your behavior in its light, and think meanwhile of the Attributes of your Lord.

The Almighty has provided us with signs that mark the unbelievers; so let's go through that in the Qur'an:
- "Yet those who reject faith hold others as equal with their Guardian-Lord." (6:1)
- "Of those who reject faith the patrons are the *taghoots*." (2:257)
- "Those who reject faith fight in the cause of the *taghoot*." (4:76)
- "This is because those who reject Allah follow vanities." (47:3)

- "The unbelievers dispute with vain argument, in order therewith to weaken the truth, and they treat My Signs as a jest, as also the fact that they are warned." (18:56)
- "Soon shall We cast terror into the hearts of the unbelievers, for that they joined companions with Allah, for which He had sent no authority: their abode will be the Fire: and evil is the home of the wrong-doers!" (3:151)
- "The unbelievers are protectors, one of another." (8:73)
- "But those who reject faith turn away from that whereof they are warned." (46:3)
- "Those who reject faith – they are the wrong-doers." (2:254)
- "The prayer of those without faith is nothing but futile wandering." (13:14)
- "If any do fail to judge by the light of what Allah has revealed, they are no better than unbelievers." (5:44)
- "And behold, We said to the angels: 'Bow down to Adam." And they bowed down: not so Iblis: he refused and was haughty: he was of those who reject faith." (2:34)
- "Don't you see that We have set the devils on against the unbelievers, to incite them with fury?" (19:83)
- "The parable of those who reject faith is as if one were to shout like a goat-herd, to things that listen to nothing but calls and cries: deaf, dumb, and blind, they are void of wisdom." (2:171)
- "Those who deny Allah and His Messengers, and those who wish to separate Allah from His Messengers, saying: 'We believe in some but reject others,' and those who wish to take a course midway – they are in truth equally unbelievers; and We have prepared for unbelievers a humiliating punishment." (4:150-151)

From an analysis of the traits and marks of unbelievers, we may draw out about them the following list:

An unbeliever:
1. Appeals to the *taghoot* for his judgment
2. Heeds the *taghoot*
3. Deaf, dumb, blind, having no wisdom
4. Holds as equal that Who has created and that who creates nothing
5. Follows vanities
6. Feels unsafe, his heart being filled with terror
7. Wrong-doing (trespassing the limits set by Allah)
8. Does not judge in the light of what Allah has revealed
9. Prostrates to Allah in spite of himself, not willingly (an example of this is Iblis)
10. Has the devil for friend
11. His intrigue appears fine to his sight, and so he is led away from the right way
12. His prayer is futile
13. He assumes that Allah has revealed different religions, and he makes distinctions among Allah's messengers, claiming that he believes in some, but not in others.
14. Does not hold as forbidden what Allah forbids
15. Follows delusion (rather than what Allah's messengers teach. For instance Moses addressed his people, forbidding them to kill. But you see how the *taghoots* of the earth send men from one war to another, seeking to kill.)

By referring to the above list, we may examine how far the qualities of an unbeliever, as given by Allah, fit the society we live in: we may in this way give our verdict whether the so called 'Islamic' society is still Islamic, or it has passed unconsciously into a state of disbelief!

One criterion of an unbeliever provided by Allah is that unbelievers take the *taghoot* for patron, and they fight in his cause. So let's consider who at present is the patron of Islamic societies:

- Is it Allah or the *taghoots* who rule?
- Do Muslims fight with and for the *taghoot*?
- Have Muslims fought the Kuwait-Iraq war, and other wars, in the cause of Allah or because the *taghoots* of the earth commanded them to?
- Do Muslims hold Allah and the *taghoot* as equal? (By saying (addressing Allah during pilgrimage): 'In obedience we come to You!' Then saying, 'We defend you, *taghoot*, with our blood and life!')
- Are Muslims' efforts fruitful, or are they in vain, blown away like chaff?
- When Muslims pray to Allah day and night: 'Give us victory over our enemies, O Lord, and destroy our foes!' does their Lord give them victory?
- Do Muslims judge in the light of what Allah has revealed? Or they judge by the dictates of their whims and desires?

If they claim to judge in the light of what Allah has revealed, why then do not they shun the *taghoot*? Have they not been commanded to shun him and to reject him? As we have seen, the meaning of 'Muslim' is a person who submits to his Lord, and Muslims do not submit: therefore they are not Muslim.

We may find support in the assertion of an eminent scholar, the late Muhammad Mutawalli Sha'rawi, when he said in a book of his, *That is Islam* (published by Dar al-Hurriyah, Cairo, Egypt): "Indeed we are no longer an Islamic society." (page 8)

So many pressing questions a Muslim (who submits) will have to pause and consider... Let him recall that Allah has defined an unbeliever, and that it is left to the individual to choose between faith and disbelief: no one, not even the prophets, are given authority over men to make them believe or disbelieve. About that we may recite in the Qur'an:

"Say: 'The truth is from your Lord.' Let him who will, believe, and let him who will, reject it." (18:29)

Allah does not command anyone to slay an unbeliever on account of his disbelief: he may only be killed for his aggression. About that we have this verse from the Qur'an:

"And the unbelievers said to their messengers: 'Be sure we shall drive you out of our land, or you shall return to our religion.' But their Lord inspired this message to them: 'Verily We shall cause the wrong-doers to perish. And verily We shall cause you to abide in the land, and succeed them. This for such as fear the time when they shall stand before My tribunal – such as fear the punishment denounced.'" (14:13-14)

That an unbeliever is so is in the hand of Allah; we are ordained to do jihad 'i.e. strive' in dealing with him, not to kill him; reflect on that in reciting the following verse from the Qur'an:

"Therefore do not listen to the unbelievers, but strive against them with the utmost strenuousness, with the Qur'an." (25:52) A believer is ordained by Allah to denounce the other if the latter rejects faith, even when he happens to be a parent, a son, one's people or tribe. That is what the Almighty Allah ordains in the following verse:

"There is for you an excellent example to follow in Abraham and those with him, when they said to their people: 'We are clear of you and of whatever you worship beside Allah: we have rejected you, and there has arisen, between us and you, enmity and hatred for ever – unless you believe in Allah and Him alone.'" (60:4)

So Abraham is here dissociating himself from people because they have rejected Allah: it is so because Allah commanded him not to be a supporter of the unbelievers, nor to be friends with them.

That Muslims nowadays assume that prayer, fasting, paying the ordained charity, pilgrimage and pronouncing the testimony are the fundamentals of Islam – is a false assumption: for all these are just a fraction of Allah's true religion as it is represented in the Holy Qur'an. The primary principle of religion is to reject *taghoot* and then to believe in Allah; we may learn that much from the following words of the Almighty:

"Whoever rejects *taghoot* and believes in Allah has grasped the most trustworthy hand-hold, that never breaks. And Allah hears and knows all things." (2:256)

Or take this other verse:

"Have you not seen those who declare that they believe in the revelations that have come to you and to those before you? Their real wish is to resort together for judgment in their disputes to the *taghoot*, though they were ordered to reject him. But Satan's wish is to lead them astray far away." (4:60)

CHAPTER SIXTEEN

An Idolater

Allah the Almighty has ordained that the site of the Sacred House of Mecca should be a tangible sign of His Oneness, to which are brought fruits of all kinds; He has ordained that visiting the Sacred House of Mecca <u>by all people</u> should be an affirmation of this Oneness. There is proof enough of this fact in the supplication pronounced by people while circumambulating the *ka'bah* (the cubic structure), for a pilgrim says: "In obedience we come to You, in obedience, for there is no partner unto You!" Some would utter this with their mouth, and they may repeat it for many times, but you do not find in their life a proof of it, for they do not realize what exactly is the meaning of 'there is no partner unto You.' You will see the individual, after he has returned to his routine life, practicing various forms of idolatry, implicitly and explicitly: it is idolatry under the pressure of a tyrannical regime, and because of indigence – that when the above supplication is an expression of the entirety of religion. You may find a proof of that in the words of the Almighty, when he says in the Qur'an:

"Behold! We gave the site, to Abraham, of the Sacred House saying: 'Do not associate anything in worship with Me; and sanctify My House for those who compass it round, or stand up, or bow, or prostrate themselves therein in prayer.'" (22:26)

Let's focus in the above verse on the Almighty's saying:
'Do not associate anything in worship with Me.'
And let's compare that with:
'There is no partner unto You, in obedience we come! (in the previous supplication)

Let's look also at another verse:

"Allah does not forgive that partners should be set up with Him; but He forgives anything less, to whom He pleases; to set up partners with Allah is to devise a sin most heinous indeed." (4:48)

Idolatry, as represented in the Holy Qur'an, is the most serious crime punishable by the Almighty Lord. There is no toleration of this sin at all. See how in the above verse He says that He will not forgive this at all; see also how He designates it as fabrication; and see how he designates it as sin, and then as heinous. He affirms elsewhere that Allah and His Messenger disavow all who ascribe divinity to aught beside Him:

"And a proclamation from Allah and His Apostle is herewith made unto all mankind on this day of the Greatest Pilgrimage: 'Allah disavows all who ascribe divinity to aught beside Him, and so does His Apostle.'" (9:3)

In various locations of the Qur'an, idolaters are described as miscreants, as trespassers, as having sold Allah's signs for a paltry price, as barring others from the way of Allah, as being the heads of disbelief, as having no binding oaths, as having plotted to expel the Messenger, as being the first to attack the believers. He forbids Muslims from giving away their daughters in marriage to idolaters; He forbids them from praying for forgiveness for the idolaters. And, last, He commands believers to fight the idolaters wherever they find them. Of no other group can one find in the

Holy Qur'an such abundance of detailed information, and with such insistence –which is a sure indication of the extraordinary significance of this issue. But, with all this unusual importance, and despite all the warnings, very few people seem to take note of it seriousness.

It may be noted that Allah does not say, 'kill the unbelievers.'

What we have is 'fight the unbelievers,' mentioned twice, once 'if they aggress against you,' and once, 'if they do not go straight in dealing with you.' It is evident that no fighting of unbelievers is to take place, unless another condition is met. Only in the case of idolatry is the Qur'anic discourse so stern.

Now about the nature of idolatry, we may say that one form of it, though undeclared, is to follow any other doctrine, or a legislator, in defiance of Allah's doctrine: even when such idolatry is disguised under a religious appearance.

Hence, for any person to assume a position of partnership with Allah in His dominion, is not pardonable, never ever: He is the King of men, the Lord of men. So that is a settled matter, never to be taken lightly.

Now, going over that impressive barrage of terms, most subtle, decisive, and firm, we may add now how this topic is enhanced with terms of remonstration, warning and threat, and distributed over the whole of the Qur'an. That serves to stress and to plainly reveal the gravity of this crime of idolatry: it is the crime of holding any one as a partner to That Who has created you. Then, believers are left no choice but to cut off relations with the idolaters, to keep quite clear of them. And that should be no wonder when we survey the following list about the fundamentals of religion:

1. That you take no partner unto Allah
2. That you devise no falsehood about Allah
3. That you commit no indecent deed
4. That you do not commit a sin
5. That you do not trespass against people wrongfully

And an idolater has violated the first and second items of these fundamentals, and as a matter of course the rest of them.

In other words, Allah ordains:

- Kill not the soul which Allah has made sacred except in the course of justice
- Withhold from people nothing which is their due
- Render back your trusts to those to whom they are due; and when you judge between man and man, you judge with justice
- Forgive and overlook
- Say to people what is good
- Do no mischief in the earth
- Do not kill your children out of want: We shall provide sustenance for you as well as for them
- Enjoin what is right, forbid what is wrong.

But an idolater wants nothing of this: he wants to be a transgressor who goes about, inflicting on Allah's salves what he wishes: sending them to wars whenever he likes, killing whoever he likes and sparing whoever he likes. He wants to deal with the environment the way he likes; to endue with honor whoever he likes, and to bring low whoever he likes; issuing a visa to whoever he likes, and expelling whoever he likes; allotting land to whoever he likes; conferring nationality on whoever he likes; supplying with water whoever he likes, and depriving of it whoever he likes. He likes to have everything in his hand: exactly as if he were a partner to Allah, and to have had a hand in creation.

It is about them that Allah says:
"And tell them that the water is to be divided between
them, each one's right to drink being brought forward."
(54:28)

If we, by way of contrast, look back at the band of the noble
messengers, across their long history, we find their message to
be one: introducing mankind to their One God, the King, the
True Lord; fulfilling their positions as slaves to Him Alone;
denouncing any lordship of the *taghoots* of the earth. Through
the words of the True God man's consciousness will come to
life, making him responsive to the messages that are harmonious
with his spirit. If, on the other hand, his consciousness accepts
what is incongruent with his spirit, a proportionate amount of
responsiveness to fruitful messages is destroyed. He will then
drift down unfathomable abysses of darkness. It is so because
what man is capable of comprehending, probing and perceiving,
is always related to his domain, to man's own limits; and
hence man's mental set up at any moment puts a limit on his
perception: should he neglect to develop that ability, he will slip
further down. Man can only survive (intellectually) in his proper
environment of consciousness, in the same way as water is the
fish's living environment.

From the above, let's go to the message of Prophet Muhammad,
whose first call was:

To give up associating any partner with Allah;
and to affirm that:
There is no god but Allah
It is not by coincidence that all the messengers of Allah were
resisted and fought against, for the above message was the very
kernel of Allah's religion.

The concept of idolatry is quite subtle, and may occur in relation with the simplest or most complex matters. Therefore, man needs to think at every step he walks: his god could be Allah, but it could be his desires, the ruler, the party, his nationality, habits, traditions, and so on. Allah has given His judgment concerning every minute or huge matter: to sidestep Allah's law and submit to another law is idolatry.

The Oneness of Allah occupies the very center of religion; and the prophets have striven to establish this concept, to pull down stone idols and to establish the eschewing of *taghoots*. And yet history shows that for every stone idol destroyed, there rose hundreds of idols disguised as nationality, race, party or people – the concept of idol has survived across the ages; if anything, more branches of it have kept emerging, and are still emerging.

The main attribute of the Deity is creation: the King of people is He Who has created them – not anyone who happens to occupy a position of tyrannizing or oppressing men. Tyranny and transgression against men are two crimes that are committed by those who harp on democracy, whereas they should have forbidden it. Tyranny is also committed by the *taghoots* of the earth, who disregard what has been forbidden by Him who created mankind. No wonder then how miserable the nations of the earth are. It is worth our while to consider some relevant verses of the Qur'an:

- "Do they indeed ascribe to Him as partners things that can create nothing, but are themselves created? No aid can they give them, nor can they aid themselves!" (7:191-192)
- "O men! Here is a parable set forth! Listen to it! Those on whom, besides Allah, you call, cannot create even a fly, if they all met together for the purpose! And if the fly should snatch away anything from them, they would

have no power to release it from the fly. Feeble are those who petition and those whom they petition. No just estimate have they made of Allah: for Allah is He Who is strong and able to carry out His Will." (22:73-74)

- "Say: 'Who is the Lord and Sustainer of the heavens and the earth?' Say: 'It is Allah.' Say: 'Do you then take for worship protectors other than Him, such as have no power either for good or for harm to themselves?' Say: 'Are the blind equal with those who see? Or the depths of darkness equal with light?' Or do they assign to Allah partners who have created anything as He has created, so that the creation seemed to them similar? Say: 'Allah is the Creator of all things: He is the One, the Supreme and Irresistible.'" (13:16)

- "Say: 'Have you seen these "partners" of yours whom you call upon besides Allah? Show me what it is they have created in the wide earth. Or have they a share in the heaven? Or have We given them a Book from which they can derive clear evidence?' – Nay, the wrong-doers promise each other nothing but delusions." (35:40)

The Muslim supposes that with the destruction of the last idol which the Bedouins used to worship, the concept of idolatry has disappeared. But in fact idolatry has entered through another gate, under a new shape. In this way many men assume they are believers when they commit idolatry, though they do it unaware. About such people we may quote the following words from the Qur'an:

"And most of them do not believe in Allah without associating others as partners with Him!" (12:106)

To return to Allah, one should be careful to fulfill this condition: that he does not take a partner to Him Who has created everything. Therefore we find the Qur'an say:

"Those who believe in the Signs of their Lord; those who do not join in worship partners with their Lord; and those who dispense their charity with their hearts full of fear, because they will return to their Lord." (23:58-60)

It is absolutely vital that one corrects his criteria of idolatry in the light of what Allah has revealed, and that is more pressing in our current time: that is because the tyrants have greatly multiplied, the 'partners' are abundant; and each goes wearing an invisible hat to conceal his real features, and to distract people's minds from his being a partner: you see the new partners come under such guises as democracy, people's rule, intellectual or spiritual freedom; and the wretched individual assumes that he has control over his life, that he is captain of his affairs; that he can even do without Allah.

Abraham cut off all relation with his people; he did not say: 'my forefathers were like that, so I should follow them.' He announced instead, 'There is no god but Allah;' dissociating himself from any currents or trends of his time. He destroyed the idols, and destroyed the relationship with his people: he eliminated from his heart any affection for those who profess enmity for Allah, until they should accept the condition of giving up idolatry. Abraham refused to obey his people, and disavowed even his father: about that Allah says in the Qur'an:

"When it became clear to him that he was an enemy of Allah, he dissociated himself from him." (9:114)

The concept of idolatry revolves on inequality: Allah has bred all people from Adam, and Adam himself was created from soil; He decreed that, as a start, we are all equal in rights and duties, in status and rank. Then He added that one's rank may rise or fall depending on man's behavior. But in an idolatry system, a man is placed above another man, an idea above man, or a party, or a race, etc. while Allah gives no one precedence over man, not even the devil: for the devil is given authority only over those who take him for protector, and not over those who believe in Allah: about that we may read the following words of the Almighty in the Qur'an:

"When you read the Qur'an, seek Allah's protection from Satan the Rejected One. He does not have any authority over those who believe and put their trust in their Lord. His authority is over those only who take him as a patron and who join partners with Allah." (16:98-100)

And generally, for any tyrant, he has no authority over those who believe. His authority is solely over those who take him for patron, a partner to Allah in His dominion. To obey the *taghoot*, to take him for a partner to Allah, detracts from man's dignity, while Allah had honored man; for the essence of idolatry is obedience, as may be supported by the following words of the Almighty:

"But the devils ever inspire their friends to contend with you; if you were to obey them, you would indeed be idolaters." (6:121)

CHAPTER SEVENTEEN

The Miscreant

A miscreant is defined by Allah as one who has turned to disbelief after having been a believer. He further describes him as one who forgets the fact that he has been created; elsewhere as being a hypocrite. But He provides us with the distinguishing feature of a miscreant when He says, as we read in the Qur'an:

"If any do fail to judge by the light of what Allah has revealed, they are the miscreants." (5:47)

And the question will occur to the mind: Do the Muslim leaders judge in accordance with what Allah has revealed? And further: Do the rest of Muslims judge in accordance with what Allah has revealed?

Let's read this other verse in the Qur'an:
"They have forgotten Allah; so He has forgotten them. Verily the hypocrites are miscreants." (9:67)

So, if Muslims shout, addressing Allah, 'In obedience we come to You,' while in Mecca; then they return to the *taghoot*'s kingdom and chant, 'In obedience to you, O king … In obedience to you, O president!' – is that hypocrisy?

To be able to judge rightly, we need first to be cognizant of what Allah has revealed: the only place for that is Allah's Scripture. We find that Allah has revealed: 'worship Allah;' while we find man either works for the *taghoot* or fights against him, both in defiance of what Allah has decreed in a succinct judgment: 'eschew him.'

So does our failure to judge in the light of what Allah has revealed turn us into miscreants? Does it turn us into hypocrites? Didn't this happen to Iblis (Satan) when Allah commanded him to do something and he rebelled against his Lord's command, and failed to obey it, as reported by the Almighty in the Qur'an:

"They bowed down except Iblis. He was one of the Jinns, and he broke the command of his Lord." (18:50)

It must be clear and evident by now that to disobey Allah's judgment is being miscreant; it is all the same if disobedience takes the shape of knowledge or ignorance, cheating or intrigue, misinterpretation, or whatever. In all cases, a miscreant is one who follows the commands of other than Allah. About this we may look at these words of the Almighty's in the Qur'an:

"Behold! Allah took the Covenant of the prophets, saying: 'I give you a Book of Wisdom; then comes to you a Messenger, confirming what is with you; you believe in him and render him help.' Allah said: 'Do you agree, and take this My Covenant as binding on you?' They said: 'We agree.' He said: 'Then bear witness, and I am with you among the witnesses.' If any turn back after this, they are miscreants. Do they seek for other than the religion of Allah?" (3:81-83)

A miscreant is one who violates the covenant between Allah and men. About that we have this in the Qur'an:

"Do not take other than Me as disposer of your affairs." (17:2)

"But He does not cause to stray except the miscreant." (2:26)

And,

"Allah does not guide the miscreant." (5:108)

About particular peoples, there is the people of Noah described as miscreants; and Pharaoh and his people, among others. Let's see that in the Qur'an:

"Now put your hand [addressing Moses] into your bosom, and it will come forth white without stain: these are among the nine Signs you will take to Pharaoh and his people: for they are a people rebellious in transgression." (27:12)

"So were the people of Noah before them for they were miscreants." (51:46)

Being miscreant happens as a result of forgetfulness. As was mentioned in the previous chapter, as fish do not survive outside water, the human spirit does not in fact survive without Allah's words. This aspect is also described in the words of the Almighty, when He says in the Qur'an:

"O you who believe! Give your response to Allah and His Messenger, when He calls you to that which will give you life; and know that Allah comes between man and his heart, and that it is He to Whom you shall all be gathered." (8:24)

A miscreant is not really alive: His forgetfulness comes from abandoning faith, and failing to practice it; therefore he is dead.

CHAPTER EIGHTEEN

Going Astray

Everybody seems to speak about going astray, and to be accusing some group of having gone astray. Almost every school of thought describes the other groups as being astray, each using their own yardstick and criteria: what one group takes to be a main component of straying is not thought so by the next group. Things have reached a point when the concept of straying is so unwieldy that it is more misleading than helpful. Our only resort, then, is to seek Allah's definition: it is extremely urgent that we seek in His words the real meaning, especially in the present circumstances of the so called 'Islamic' societies. Allah reminds us, in the following verse from the Qur'an, that it is He who knows who is astray:

"For your Lord knows best, who have strayed from His Path, and who receive guidance." (16:125)

Definition of the Straying Person:

A straying person is defined by Allah in the following verses of the Qur'an's:

- "But whoever changes from Faith to unbelief, has strayed without doubt from the even way." (2:108)
- "If one disobeys Allah and His Messenger, he has clearly gone astray." (33:36)

- "Those who reject Faith and keep off men from the Way of Allah, have verily strayed far, far away from the Path." (4:167)
- "One who joins other gods with Allah, has strayed far, far away from the right." (4:116)

Going astray is to take an enemy of Allah's for patron; that is clear in the following words of Allah:

"O you who believe! Take not My enemies and yours as friends or protectors – offering them your love, even though they have rejected the Truth that has come to you, and have on the contrary driven out the Prophet and yourselves from your homes because you believe in Allah your Lord! If you have come out to strive in My Way and to seek My Good Pleasure, take them not as friends, holding secret converse of love and friendship with them: for I know full well all that you conceal and all that you reveal. And any of you that does this has strayed from the Straight Path." (60:1)

Going astray is indeed a definite process, and it is summed up in moving from belief to disbelief: both disbelief and belief have been defined in previous chapters: the definition of disbelief must be clear by now, and belief too. Allah explains that taking partners with Him, driving people away from His Path, disobeying Him, and replacing belief with disbelief – these are the components of straying, and they cause perdition, humiliation and slavery in the earth. To take the *taghoot* as equal to Allah, and to accept to replace Allah's system with that of the *taghoot*, in the land that belongs only to Allah, is the very essence of man's going astray. It is helpful in understanding this to read some verses of the Qur'an:

"Then they will be thrown headlong into the Fire – they and those straying in evil, and the whole hosts of Iblis together. They will say there in their mutual bickerings: 'By Allah, we were truly in error manifest, when we held you as equals with the Lord of the Worlds; and our seducers were only those who were steeped in guilt.'" (26:94:99)

It is unfortunate that man should forget that Allah has warned him thus:

"Nor follow the desires of people who went astray in times gone by – who misled many, and strayed themselves from the even Way." (5:77)

It is in order here to remind the reader of the pivotal concept of:

Worship Allah **AND** esc hew the *taghoot*.

It is such a central point that, to ignore it is to sow the seed of straying from the path. Allah has commanded man to eschew the *taghoot*, and man has not obeyed Allah in this; therefore he was led astray. Just a simple but solid law, it is the law of 'if and only if:'

If man obeys the *taghoot* ⟶ Allah will let him go astray

Man has held the *taghoot* as partner to Allah. He has gone even further: he has brushed aside Allah's law, and followed the law of the *taghoot*. Allah commands man not to kill, except when it is right: and He defines what 'right' means: It is not in defense of self, nor country; nor for protecting the *taghoot*'s throne; nor expanding his kingdom; nor for commercial domination in the earth; nor for the advantage of companies that belong to the *taghoot*'s allies. Man has forgotten Allah's command, and so Allah has let him go astray: that indeed is straying manifest. Man does forget that the apparent power of *taghoot* is just a delusion, only a fake, for he is incapable of causing man any harm or benefit; we may learn as much from the words of the Almighty in the Qur'an, when He says:

"If you follow right guidance, no hurt can come to you from those who stray." (5:105)

When hurt does come to me, it is not caused by the *taghoot*, but by my ignorance of the right way, which causes my not following it. What I should do is to find the way: not to kill the *taghoot* or his minions. I should rather keep clear of them; for the *taghoot* will destroy himself. That also has been told us by the Almighty Lord, when He says in the Qur'an:

"Feeble indeed is the cunning of Satan." (4:76)

And, we may further rehearse in this connection:
"What! When a single disaster smites you, although you smote your enemies with one twice as great, do you say? – 'Whence is this?' Say to them: 'It is from yourselves.'" (3:165)

The problem of Muslims today is in fact that they do not believe the words of Allah, but believe the words of the *taghoot*-controlled imams or scholars, who say that our crises are caused by Israel or America, by imperialism, economy, poverty, etc. They would find everything or everyone accountable but themselves! That when Allah admonishes us: 'It is from yourselves;' 'and also in your own selves. Will you not then see?' And He warns those who do not see, do not hear, do not comprehend, do not know. And Allah tells believers:

"Victory comes only from Allah, the Mighty, the Wise." (3:126)

While the ruler-controlled scholars assert that victory comes from America, the superpower. It is such a ridiculous situation!

In the above-quoted verse, (5:105), the Qur'an has put forward this 'if and only if' relation in the following way:

If you follow right guidance, ⟶ no hurt can come to you from those who stray.

Indeed, the Qur'an is in its entirety a tightly knit network: its chapters consist of verses of established meaning, elaborated by the Wise, the Ever-Cognizant. It follows that we need to ascertain the links between things, how for instance eschewing is linked to straying; how Allah's guidance has the effect of breaking up that magic which is called the *taghoot*'s power and dominance. In proof of that we may quote from the Qur'an:

"Whosoever follows My guidance, will not lose his way, nor fall into misery." (20:123)

So let me stop a moment here and rewrite the above verse in accordance with the law of 'if and only if':

If man follows Allah's guidance ⟶ man will not fall into misery

It is right to inquire here, given the bitter nature of the actual state of things: Is a Muslim now having a life of misery, or is he contented and his efforts produce the outcome expected of them? Let's think of the answer in light of the following words of the Almighty's:

"The prayer of those without Faith is nothing but futile wandering in the mind." (13:14)

For we all see how on every Friday, and in all the mosques of the earth, the imams of 'Muslims' pray to their Lord:

"Destroy our enemy, O our Lord; put right our affairs; give us victory; give victory to the fighters in Your Cause, in Your land and in Your sea; let our revenge scourge those who have oppressed us; give victory to our rulers, and guide them, etc."

But has Allah answered your prayer? Yours, or your imams?

Is your prayer only in vain? Isn't it as Allah describes in another verse:

"The parable of those who reject their Lord is that their works are as ashes, on which the wind blows furiously on a tempestuous day: no power have they over anything that they have earned: that is the straying far, far from the good." (14:18)

Are the proceedings of Islamic and Arab summit conferences like ashes on which the wind blows furiously on a tempestuous day? Or are such meetings steps on the way of putting things right and elevating the Muslim society?

It must be manifest, then, why our enterprises bring only loss, and why our efforts are not to our advantage! Why they are all like scattered motes. It must be clear, too, why Muslims are in this state of humiliation and degradation. It is true what the True God has said of the likes of them:

"These are they who have bartered guidance for error: but their traffic is profitless, and they have lost true direction." (2:16)

That man's direction is changed from faith to disbelief is in itself straying; one aspect of that state is that man despairs of the Creator of all being, in the same way as the unbelievers despair of those in the graves. It is as Allah has said:

"But those who reject faith after they accepted it, and then go on adding to their defiance of faith – never will their repentance be accepted; for they are those who have gone astray." (3:90)

Also is revealing what Abraham said, as reported in the Qur'an:

"And who despairs of the mercy of his Lord, but such as go astray?" (15:56)

It will not avail man to bite at his hands in remorse and regret, for the Almighty says:

"The Day that the wrong-doer will bite at his hands, he will say: 'O! would that I had taken a straight path with the Messenger! Ah! Woe is me! Would that I had never taken such a one for a friend! He did lead me astray from the Message of Allah after it had come to me! Ah! The devil is but a traitor to man!' Then the Messenger will say: 'O my Lord! Truly my people took this Qur'an for just foolish nonsense.'" (25:27-30)

And you see how many Muslims have taken the *taghoot*-controlled imams for masters and guides.

Think of Adam's son who, as reported in the Qur'an (5:28), said to his killing-intent brother: "Even if you stretch out your hand against me to kill me, I shall not stretch out my hand against you to kill you, for I fear Allah, Lord of the Worlds." And see how Muslims are divided into Sunnis and Shiites, killing one another.

I leave it to you to decide if the Sunnis and Shiites are the (spiritual) descendants of Abel or Cain? And to decide if, when they slay one another, they are adhering to the way of guidance or straying?

CHAPTER NINETEEN

The Unheeding

The Almighty says:

"Their reckoning draws nigh for mankind, while they turn away in heedlessness." (21:1)

A heedless person is one who is forgetful of Him Who created him; who is unmindful of Who he must direct his face to; unmindful of what makes him direct his face somewhere. He is forgetful of the fact that when he chooses his direction, that must not be for the sake of position, or material gain, or for any advantage: It must be only for the sake of Allah. With the beats of his heart, he should be murmuring: 'It is You, my Lord, Who Are my destination, and Your pleasure is what I seek!' He should have not followed his desires, so that his case should not go out of hand. He has to be mindful of all that, and never to be unheeding.

A certain poet complains, in the following couplets, about the lack of such mindful individuals:

I met the old man, searching diligently, lamp in hand;
Walking in every possible direction;
Groaning meanwhile: 'I'm fed up with encountering only
    sheep and cattle;
Is there a real man to be found anywhere?'

'We have already searched,' his companions said, 'it is the
   impossible you seek.'
'But then,' he said, 'it is that impossible I still search for.'

To weigh yourself and others, seek no balance except that
of Allah: that is a balance indeed! So let's ask here, how does He
define the unheeding? Let's find that in the Qur'an:

1. They have hearts wherewith they understand not
2. eyes wherewith they see not
3. and ears wherewith they hear not.
4. They are like the cattle – nay more misguided:
5. for they are heedless
(7:179)

Allah does not destroy towns unawares: for Allah is not unjust to
His slaves. He does destroy people who reject truth; because they
turn their face from Him, and because they are heedless of His
Signs. That is what happened to Pharaoh and his people. In the
words of the Qur'an:

"But every time We removed the penalty from them according
to a fixed term which they had to fulfill – behold! They broke the
word! So We exacted retribution from them: We drowned them
in the sea, because they rejected Our Signs, and were heedless
about them." (7:135-136)

It is a constant law of Allah, the Almighty. Let's read a little
more about that:

"Those who behave arrogantly on the earth in defiance of
right – I will turn them away from My Signs: Even if they see all
the Signs, they will not believe in them; and if they see the way
of right conduct, they will not adopt it as the way; but if they see

the way of error, that is the way they will adopt. For they have rejected Our Signs, and were heedless of them." (7:146)

And, last, let's look at these verses:

"Think not that Allah does not heed the deeds of those who do wrong. He but gives them respite against a Day the reckoning will be established. They running forward with necks outstretched, their heads uplifted, their gaze returning not toward them, and their hearts a gaping void!" (14:42-43)

CHAPTER TWENTY

The Tidings

In the midst of total darkness live ignorant masses; no real debate, interaction, or communication; a state of stagnation, foolish exchanges, mutual denouncements and negative attitudes; conflicts and wars are waged everywhere; and you hear a big claim about the rights of man. In broad daylight, and under the eyes of mankind – men are massacred, rights go down the drain; nations are subdued, property is confiscated, women are raped: and yet the imams see nothing and hear nothing!

Self-criticism is crucial for correcting man's march in the earth. It is not palatable in the consciences of honest people, wherever they happen to be (Those who listen and heed), to keep their silence when any human being is exposed to a hurt anywhere in the world: no matter whether the hurt is inflicted in the name of religion, democracy, freedom, or any other cause. Those who trumpet for democracy have, in the folds of their rhetoric, something they call allowing religion to be, although they themselves have no faith in religion. And then they make big claims about their giving people the freedom of conviction, as if they are a great god that is bestowing his bounty on his slaves to be worshipped. They tell people that they have granted them their freedom, that they stripped them of that – though they sit on the necks of people. But people do wrong themselves. That is what we learn from the following verse of the Qur'an:

"Do the unbelievers think that they can take My servants as protectors besides Me?" (18:102)

Now when those who trumpet for allowing religion to exist, after having emptied it of its content, it is worth man's while to inquire what impels those people to speak loudly about that? It is here that lies the crux of tyranny and enslaving men all over the earth; here we find people who speak but do not practice: it is those same people who support the *taghoots* of the earth, by working in their service; and if they do rebel against them, you see the troops of 'democracy' marching on people, killing them in the name of ridding the country of the tyrant, speaking at the same time about freedom and human rights, meaning of course that what is freedom for them is tyranny for the other. They can only do that since they take man to be so foolish that he cannot distinguish between the big claims of democracy and the crimes it perpetrates everywhere in the earth. That man suffers hunger and thirst is a result of the united front of democracy and tyranny, and that is because of their assumption that man is everywhere foolish: while they assert that all men are equal, they take a foolish man to be inferior to others. That is their double dealing; and they keep harping on the string of democracy; and even the down-trodden chants its name on his death-bed. At the same time, the crooked tycoons support this situation: they urge people to donate to the campaigns of those figures. The reality of course is that they go out to rob people of their money, and love to be praised for things they have not done – but they will not be in safety from the doom: Allah is ever watchful; nor is He unmindful of what those people do.

The world which adopts democracy represents religion as something opposed to intellectual freedom: and the purpose of this claim is to sow the seeds of dissatisfaction about religion among mankind: it is so because the *taghoots* of the earth know quite well that true religion represents danger for them – tyranny and oppression are forbidden in religion, and these two are the very lifeblood of the *taghoot* anywhere on the earth. Such problems of the world as hiding behind religion are really conflicts about benefits and tyranny: the *taghoots* of the earth prefer to wear the cloak of religion, patriotism, or democracy, with the intent of enslaving the multitudes. It is true to call democracy a political game, since in such a game one *taghoot* falls down to be only replaced by another *taghoot* (in the appearance of political, religious, or national parties); and they one and all intend to enslave men. And yet, let's have hope, for truth is stronger, and it will last after them all, even if evil seems to flourish; and even if it goes unnoticed or seems to take root. We say that in the light of the following verses from the Qur'an:

"It was not Allah who oppressed them: they oppressed their own souls. The parable of those who like protectors other than Allah is that of the spider, who builds to itself a house; but truly the flimsiest of houses is that of the spider's house – if they but knew. Verily Allah knows of every thing whatever they call upon besides Him: and He is Exalted in power, Wise. And such are the parables We set forth for mankind, but only those understand them who have knowledge." (29:40-43)

Now for the emergence of a man with true convictions, honest spirit, and steadfast resolution; for a realization of the values of goodness, justice for every single man on the globe, anywhere on the globe: it is vital that those in chains be released; that consciences be released from the bonds of racism, nationalism, partisan spirit; that those who exploit religion for special interests and advantages are exposed: I mean those who faun on authority and the *taghoot*-controlled scholars. Man's dignity must be protected; his right in good life must be maintained: that no one is permitted to oppress him. It is then that the earth emerges as home for love, peace and harmony. Truly, this world is a temple that points to the One God, the Hope of all.

That the earth is at present divided into many countries and mini-countries is for the benefit of the lords of the earth, its *taghoots*, and their bootlickers. All of these are passing out of fashion, for the earth, the whole of the earth, is not theirs, as we learn from a verse of the Qur'an's:

"My servants, the righteous, shall inherit the earth." (21:105)

At the same time, to fragment the earth into countries and mini-countries runs counter to Divine law; it does not fit the innate nature of man, nor man's primary interests of cooperation, free exchange and acquaintance between the children of the human family: We say that believing in man and in his rights; he is entitled to being helped and released from the dominance, from all types of exploitation and oppression: he is slave to none but Allah.

We need to have a fresh look at religion: religion is not just abstract conviction, independent of existence. It is, on the contrary, a close interaction, awareness of and relationship between Him Who created and His creation; a relation with the world: it is a relationship between consciousness and the whole of existence. The most vital part of the relationship is the bond between man and his fellow men, a relationship based on values and ethics; aiming at a joint effort for building a better world, a world governed by the values of truth, justice and dignity.

About that, let's reflect on these couplets:

Should a people's loss be in their morality,
Then you may well announce their death.
If you crave success in all your affairs,
Then start with adopting good morality, and the rest will
be fine.

It is so because a soul is given the best when it chooses
the best conduct;
It is given the very vilest, when it chooses evil ways.

It is a grave moral crime when religion is tampered with: so
let's accept truth as our common reference; and let's agree that
if one party is on right guidance the other must be in manifest
error. I pray to our Lord that He bring all mankind to accept
truth. What we need for successful debate is that debaters meet in
love, that each gets over his fanaticism, completely and decisively.
When I say that I do it because I fully realize that I am no more
than a servant of the Almighty Allah: if I am a true servant of
Allah, I must wish for you what I wish for myself. And when
honesty emanates from my words, and I deal with the other with
love, I will be listening to him attentively: and he will be sure to
listen to me. A lot of discretion and tact must be there of course,
for such debates to get ahead. Am I talking sense? I may not be
using the happiest words, but my aim is right.

I learn this from such verses of the Qur'an as the following:

"Allah does not forbid you, with regard to those who do not
fight you for your faith nor drive you out of your homes, from
dealing kindly and justly with them: for Allah loves those who
are just." (60:8)

When a call to love and cooperation is heard; when working
for mutual good becomes a habit; when such an atmosphere is
accepted – you may be sure that we have built a strong fortress
for mankind.

There must be a new rebirth of man, who is at present torn
between contending powers. It must be admitted that ignorance
is the enemy of debate; and we must get over that hurdle to
knowledge and ignoring of others. To realize a state of mutual

respect, we need to know each other, truly and deeply: from there we can set together to wide horizons of debate. There will be then a good chance that the human mind will have a true conception of things, and man will be enabled to implement such conception in his life – to the extent that man comprehends the words of Jesus and the Qur'an. Man will find in both sources a great wealth of wisdom and food for the mind; and he will need to reflect long on both.

It is a delusion and a myth to assume that there is Islam as distinct from Christianity, as two different systems. It is a delusion to imagine that the church can turn Muslims into Christians; it is a delusion, too, to imagine that Islam requires Christians to be Muslim, by changing their religion. Christ was a Muslim, and Muhammad inherited Christ.

Let me repeat:

Christ, peace be upon him, was a Muslim (meaning: he submitted to Allah.)

Muhammad, peace be upon him, inherited Christ, peace be upon him.

By comparing the sayings and deeds of Christ, peace be upon him, with Allah's Scriptures, revealed to Muhammad, peace be upon him, as inscribed in the Holy Qur'an, one will conclude the truthfulness of Christ. That for one thing. One will also notice how far from accurate is religion in people's minds. But unfortunately, we face here a double catastrophe: on the one hand people do not well understand what Scriptures are inscribed in the Holy Qur'an; and do not, on the other, understand the sayings of Christ, peace be upon him.

Take up what the Messenger, peace be upon him, left behind, the Holy Qur'an.

Take it up, and compare it with what Christ, peace be upon him, said, as you find it in the Holy Bible: you will then agree with me. If you understand who Christ, peace be upon him, was, I can tell you who Muhammad, peace be upon him, was. The Qur'an is a complex discourse, in which five sciences intertwine; and the sayings of Christ, peace be upon him, provide one with the right senses of the Qur'an. Therefore I say that both Muslims and Christians misunderstand religion: it is a conception that runs counter to what they hold in their hands; and in this way they are self-contradictory, though they do not realize it.

CHAPTER TWENTY ONE

The Condemned

As warding off Allah's wrath is a most vital need of man, as it is absolutely important – one can hardly express the ample grace embodied in Allah's demonstrating to His servants what wins His pleasure, and what provokes His wrath. There is no bounty as precious as this. A certain mystic poet has tried to express this grace; she said (addressing the Lord):

I don't care when You are well-disposed if life is bitter;
Nor do I care when You are contented if people are wrathful;
When You and I are on good terms,
I don't care if the whole world is indignant;
As long as Your goodwill is intact, all is easy;
For all that is above earth, is earth.

One people that incurred Allah's wrath were the Children of Israel; and wretchedness was their portion: "That is because (as the Qur'an tells us):

1. They rejected the Signs of Allah
2. and slew the prophets in defiance of right
3. this is because they rebelled
4. and transgressed beyond bounds.

5. Not all of them are alike: of the People of the Book are a portion that stand for the right; they rehearse the revelations of Allah all night long, and they prostrate themselves in adoration. They believe in Allah and the Last Day; they enjoin what is right, and forbid what is wrong; and they hasten in emulation in all good works; they are in the ranks of the religious. Of the good that they do, nothing will be rejected of them; for Allah knows well those that do right."
(3:112-115)

As you see, Allah recounts in detail what it is that has incurred Allah's anger against the Children of Israel, and that is for others to take note and ward off Allah's wrath.

And yet, the imam has implanted into the minds of his congregation that 'the condemned' is an indelible mark of the Children of Israel, in the same way as 'the straying' is an indelible mark of the followers of Christ. Such reasoning is paired with the conviction that the followers of Muhammad are chosen, for the mere fact that they say with their mouths, 'We are Muslims.' So who are the condemned? What the imam says is falsified by the words of Allah as we shall see. Allah says that any of the following five features distinguishes the condemned:

1. Murder, in the light of Allah's saying:
   "If a man kills a believer intentionally, his recompense is Hell, to abide therein for ever: and the wrath and the curse of Allah are upon him, and a dreadful penalty is prepared for him." (4:93)
2. Idolatry and hypocrisy, in the light of Allah's saying:
   "And that He may punish the hypocrites, men and women, and the polytheists, men and women, who imagine an evil opinion of Allah. On them is a round of evil: the wrath of Allah is on them: He has cursed them

and got Hell ready for them: and evil is it for destination."
(48:6)

3. Transgression, in the light of Allah's saying:
    "Eat of the good things We have provided for your
    sustenance, but commit no excess therein, lest My wrath
    should justly descend on you: and those on whom
    descends My wrath, do perish indeed!" (20:81)

4. Taking for friends a people whom Allah condemns:
    "Have you not seen those who turn in friendship to such
    as have the wrath of Allah upon them: they are neither of
    you nor of them, and they swear to falsehood knowingly."
    (58:14)

5. Inventing falsehood or taking the *taghoot* for patron:
    "Those who took the calf for worship will indeed be
    overwhelmed with wrath from their Lord, and with
    shame in this life: thus do We recompense those who
    invent falsehoods." (7:152)

CHAPTER TWENTY TWO

The Truth-Rejecters

There is a difference between a liar and a truth-rejecter; there is a difference, too, between a lying person and a liar, for the latter is wont to tell lies. It is also true that one may disbelieve, but then may get further into disbelief until he is an unbeliever.

From this we inquire: Who is a truth-rejecter?

He is a person who invents lies which he attributes to Allah, meaning to confound truth with falsehood, and ultimately to defeat truth, to cling to falsehood: he is thereby disbelieving in Allah's grace. Truth, however, is something stable and constant – never will anyone be able to replace it with another system that will overwhelm truth, and will be equally provable.

So let's find our cue about the truth-rejecters in the Qur'an, and we find there that the Almighty says:

"It is those who do not believe in the Signs of Allah, that forge falsehood: it is they who lie!" (16:105)

An inventor of lies which he attributes to Allah is an unbeliever, or a wrong-doer, which we also learn from the Qur'an:

"All food was lawful to the Children of Israel, except what Israel made unlawful for itself, before the Law (of Moses) was revealed. Say: 'You bring the Law and study it, if you be men of truth.' If they, after this, invent a lie and attribute it to Allah, they are indeed unjust wrong-doers. Say: 'Allah speaks the Truth: follow the religion of Abraham, the sane in faith; he was not of the idolaters.'" (3:93-95)

Now although I did, in my previous book, define a sign, it is in order that I repeat this definition here: for the meaning of this word is the key to defining a truth-rejecter.

A sign is a distinguishing mark, a material trace that is amenable to observation and examination. Should we be studying a crime of murder, and should we find a sign, material evidence, that proves the death of the suspect ten years before the occurrence of the crime, then this sign proves the suspect's innocence of the crime: how can he be the murderer when the crime took place today, and the suspect died ten years ago? So what we have here is a sign, material evidence, or proof. Now a truth-rejecter invents a lie, by rejecting a sign, a sign that can be proved by a person who knows the truth.

A sign is a pointer, by which a believer finds his way. Every time a fresh sign is brought to a believer's notice, he will be steadier in faith. As for an unbeliever, he will say: 'What does Allah mean by this fresh parable?'

About this situation, the Almighty say:
"Say: 'Travel through the earth and see what was the end of those who rejected truth.'" (6:11)

Allah is telling man to take a lesson from the mistakes of others. That is again what we learn from another verse:

"Say: 'Travel through the earth and see what was the end of those before you.'" (30:42)

CHAPTER TWENTY THREE

The Transgressors

The Almighty Lord defines a transgressor as one who barters Allah's signs for a little price; that he hinders people from the Way of Allah; that he does not honor the ties of kinship or of pacts; and he practices lying. About all the above, let's go to the Qru'an:

"How can there be a league with them, seeing that if they get an advantage over you, they do not respect in you the ties either of kinship or covenant? With fair words from their mouths they entice you, but their hearts are averse from you; and most of them are rebellious and wicked. They have sold the Signs of Allah for a miserable price, and many have they hindered from His Way: evil indeed are the deeds they have done. In a believer they do not respect the ties either of kinship or covenant! It is they who have transgressed all bounds." (9:8-10)

Transgression here is of course going beyond the bounds set by Allah, and nothing else. A transgressor of the bounds is a wrong-doer; and a wrong-doer is an unbeliever. That is what we learn from the Qur'an:

"Do cast into Hell every
contumacious
rejecter of Allah –

who forbade what was good,
transgressed all bound,
cast doubts and suspicions." (50:24-25)

Allah seals the heart of this person, in retribution for his transgression; Allah will not wrong any one: it is men who wrong themselves. And after a heart is sealed, it will not respond to what man sees or hears. Therefore, a human soul has two ways: that it keeps away from wrong-doing, and that is the way of fearing Allah; and the other is the way of the devil, when man chooses doing wrong. But even after one has chosen the way of doing wrong, he still has two options: that he repent and returns to Allah, then accept willingly to inflict retribution on himself. The other option is that he wades further into the way of wrong-doing, reaping all the fruit he can of his wrong-doing: this last state is the one described in the Qur'anic expression, quoted above: 'They bartered the Signs of Allah for a little price." As for punishment, it is for healing the human spirit, so that it realizes the enormity of its deeds. When Allah punishes a spirit, He does so for curing it, for He is the All-knowing, the All-cognizant. O our Lord! No knowledge do we have except that which You teach us. It is real wretchedness that one decides to reap the fruit of his wrong-doing: while the happiest of people is he who knows that Allah is Generous, and so he endeavors to get of His bounty; who knows that Allah is Just, and so he keeps clear of wrong-doing; and even if he does wrong, he repents and atones for his wrong-doing: he will forgive others and have mercy for people, for Allah is Most Kind and Most Merciful to people; he realizes that he has no knowledge save that which he learns from the All-embracing, the All-knowing.

Looking at the messengers of Allah, you find that they were aware of all that, that they were cognizant of Allah's law, which admits no change, and no turning away. When Muhammad, peace be upon him, entered Mecca in victory, he told the Meccans: 'Go where you wish, for you are free!' Joseph, too, told his brothers, who had thrown him down the well,

"This day let no reproach be cast on you: Allah will forgive you, and He is the Most Merciful of those who show mercy!" (the Qur'an, 12:92)

Jesus, peace be upon him, said:

"Love your enemies, do good to them which hate you." (Luke, 6:27) It is so because Allah's messengers understood the law of the Almighty.

Jesus, peace be upon him, says:

"The world cannot hate you: but me it hateth, because I testify of it, that the works thereof are evil." (John, 7:7) Which indicates that Allah did not reveal one religion for the Jews and another for the followers of Christ: the Jews rejected Christ because he testified that their works were evil.

But why did he testify that their works were evil? It is so because Christ, peace be upon him, realized that it was a duty to expose straying or wrong-doing, in order to give pain to the sinner, so that he might repent and be cured. The human soul is certainly prone to evil, unless Lord bestows His Mercy.

CHAPTER TWENTY FOUR

Changing

With all the straying rampant, with continual search, with the pressure of the realities of our world, with the approaching attack, you see the world in a state of incessant dispute concerning change: that took place after the world failed in reviving the sciences of religion, and after concluding that Islam was a captive. Some assume that the trouble is in the absence of democracy, that by adopting democracy we shall be fine. Some others assume that the trouble lies in people's defeated attitude towards the pressures of the World Bank, and the absence of a powerful *taghoot*. Others still assume that the bane of our existence is Israel and imperialism; and our cure lies in eliminating them. Before that, some used to say that the Ottomans were the culprit; still before, it was said that the mamluks were the real trouble. And before that, it was said that the Arab sultans were the cause of our suffering. And now we see the *taghoot*-controlled scholars, in their two versions: those who sit in the *taghoot*'s lap, and those who would like to assassinate him, are responsible for our agony. Also are responsible the advocates of compromises, those who harp on democracy and human rights. And the list of devised solutions goes on. To the above groups you may add the advocates of racism or nationalism: but all of these groups, and those before, and those before – for fourteen centuries, soon after the Messenger passed away, are in endless bickering and fighting: they are in a vortex of misguidance, with no outlet in sight. It is Satan that makes their deed appear alluring in their eyes; and so they entice others away from the right way; they are deaf, dumb and blind: they grope in deep darkness, until such time as Allah, Lord of the Worlds, wills that they escape.

Let's turn our attention from that to a sick person who comes to see the doctor at a hospital. Of course, the first thing the doctor will ask him is:

"What brings you here?
"What is wrong with you? What is your complaint?"

The doctor does not jump to conclusions. That is because he wards off two causes of failure: time, and needless effort. If the disease gets along to its natural end, before proper intervention stops it, it is all over with the patient, and he will die and the doctor will have failed. The other enemy is needless effort: The doctor needs to save the patient and the institution unnecessary tests or examinations: If the patient has no fractured bone, and has not had an accident, if the pain is in his chest, there is no need to send him to have the bones of his limbs x-rayed. And when the symptoms and signs seem to indicate trouble in the heart, then the doctor will try to locate the trouble and order certain examinations which will help to make him sure about the disease. He is conscious of the need to make a decision concerning what is to be done in the light of the information available to him. He will be thinking at the same time of his responsibility, what he will be held accountable for: he is working against time. Often, if he feels that the case is beyond his skill and specialty, he will pass responsibility to someone else by referring the patient to another specialist. He does that because of his sense of responsibility. Now as for those who blame democracy or imperialism, or defeatism, or whatever else: they are all evading their responsibility, although they are all like that doctor.

They should ask first of all:
Where does the trouble lie?
What is the trouble?
What is the way out?
How can the patient heal?

When a carpenter is at a loss what he should do about some carpentry work, his case is not like a layman's who does not know what he should do about a similar work. The former lacks one thing: a solution to the work in hand.

The latter lacks two things:
Learning the job of carpentry; plus, learning a solution to the work in hand.

Let's then go more systematically. Let's begin by asking:

1. Where does the trouble lie?

The answer is: It lies in our selves. For evidence, you may reflect on the following words of the Almighty's:

"As also in your own selves: will you not then see?" (51:21)
"It is from yourselves." (3:165)
"Reproach your own souls." (14:22)
"If you follow right guidance, no hurt can come to you from those who stray." (5:105)

Reproach your own souls; in your own selves; from yourselves; if you follow right guidance, no hurt can come to you from those who stray. Muslims do recite all the above verses, and then they say: It is Israel; it is America; it is colonization; it is democracy.

Why cannot man distinguish between that who calls to him to flatter him, and that who calls to him to lead him to the One Who will cure him? For the Healer is Allah. When I am ill, it is

He who cures me. It is he Who gives me food and drink. It is He Who, I hope, will forgive me my faults on the Day of Judgment. It is He and not the *taghoots* of the earth; not democracy; not the mamluks; and not the Arab sultans.

The trouble, then, is in our selves.

2. What is the trouble like?

It is hypocrisy, hypocrisy, hypocrisy.

And what are its symptoms? Here are some (all drawn from the Qur'an):

- You think them to be a whole, while their hearts are divers.
- They say with their mouths that which is not in their hearts: (With our life, with our blood, we are ready to defend you, O *taghoot*!)
- Allah has sealed their hearts, and so they do not hear.
- They satisfy you with their mouths, while their hearts refuse.
- They do not understand.

3. What is the way out?

It is to expel the hypocrite from your home, even if he is a member of your family. Do not you see how when Noah, peace be upon him, said to the Lord, 'My son is of my family, and Your promise is true;' his Lord replied: 'O Noah! He is not of your family; do not ask of Me that of which you have no knowledge!'

For a more comprehensive description of the hypocrite, the reader may refer to the chapter focusing on him, where he can find ten distinguishing features of that type.

4. What is the way to healing?

That you shun the *taghoot*: do not work for him; and do not fight him. Then you sever relations with those of your family who are hypocrites, those who work for the *taghoot*, or you find one feature of the hypocrite in them. You do not obey them. Do not hurt them, but put your trust in Allah. Do jihad with the Qur'an the best you can; be rough to them; and then put your trust in the Healer.

In the present whirlwind, many people sacrifice their life and their property, assuming that they are doing a good thing. But all that they do is blown away; and they end up as losers. Their efforts are in vain, though they assume to be of those who have done a good thing. Their minds are sealed, not remembering Allah; their eyes are shut, their ears are deaf: it is so since they believe that it is with the sword that truth is distinguished from falsehood, that the sword is more truthful than the Books of Allah: that is Satan's lesson which they have learned. But they live among contradictions and paradoxes, though they cannot see that. See how they are intoxicated with the singing of Um Kalthoom, who exhorts them not to think about times gone by, nor about things not yet there: she urges them instead to capture the present moment, and enjoy it fully! And the same hypocrites are intoxicated with the recitation from the Qur'an of Abdul-Baset, the renowned sheik, as he recites to them, "Although the Hereafter is better and more lasting." (87:17)

That a hypocrite does not understand the contradictions in his life is really natural, because the first feature of this type of character is that he does not understand.

The real obstacle in the way of people is that Satan does make their work seem alluring to them, and in this way he hinders them from the right path. It is true that the Almighty Allah does cause some people to go astray; but causing man to go astray is a cause-related matter: it is done according to a Divine law. Let's get some light about that from the Qur'an:

"Allah does not guide such as are false and ungrateful." (38:3)

Man is let to go astray by Allah when he is rebellious, as we find in another verse:

"But he does not cause to stray, except those who are miscreants." (2:26)

A miscreant is someone who breaks the covenant of Allah after it is ratified, and who sunders what Allah has ordered to be joined, and does mischief on earth. What Allah orders to be joined is that people may not rip apart Allah's single religion into three religions, Christian, Muslim and Judaic: Allah's religion is one; and those who want to separate between Allah and His messengers, those who want to follow a midway between them: those are real unbelievers.

When man goes to Mecca to say, addressing Allah, "In obedience we come to You; in obedience;" then he comes back to shout, "In obedience, O *Taghoot* of the earth; with our blood we defend you, with our souls!" such falsehood and hypocrisy, most manifest to any onlooker, is the real disease of this *ummah*. The other disease is that the honest do not announce their withdrawal from the first group, when they recite in the Book of Allah, "King of men, Lord of men." The latter call themselves Muslim; but Al-Sha'rawi, the late sheikh, announced, 'We are not real Muslims.' Man does not see that the trouble is in his soul; he sees it as far from him: that is so when Allah says, "And in your own selves: Cannot you see?"

Man must realize that falsehood will vanish by itself from a consciousness the moment truth settles in it. So the words of Allah are true, but they wait for man to be aware of them; to rediscover Allah's words before it is too late. As was said above, man's present problem is in hypocrisy, which debars his sight from seeing truth. As long as man accepts a false condition, that condition will itself pull him in a direction opposite to truth: he will grope in dense and compound darkness, darkness that he cannot dispel. It is so because his acts are made alluring, and so he thinks they are good. But when Allah deems that someone should go astray, no one can guide him to the right way. It does not take great penetration to notice how hypocrisy and falsehood characterize most Muslims. It is enough for one to refer to the ten features of a hypocrite that I copied from the Holy Qur'an to be sure of the truth of what I say here. Or he may look at the traits of unbelievers, also listed in the proper chapter.

The question is now, after we realize what the trouble is — what should be my behavior, being a Muslim, submitting and dedicated?

Should I be among those who listen to words and then follow the best meaning in them? Am I among those who have been guided by Allah? Or do I hear and do nothing? Do I let myself be forgetful of Allah, in which case He will send me a devil to be my companion?

That is really the crux of the matter.

I personally have my answer, but I do not know your answer, my dear brother, and my dear sister. If your answer is: 'I hear and obey what Allah commands,' then you are my dear brother or sister; it honors me to have you for brother or sister. If not, then stay away from me – let it not occur to you that any bond of the kind of nationality, race, or party can bring us together. I reject such convictions, for I say: My Lord is Allah. So choose your position, for I have chosen my position. Every honest person in the world has chosen his or her position. It is like two trains that every day get farther and farther from each other; nay, they get farther apart by the minute. But the appointment for all is the Hour of Judgment, and that Hour will be most grievous and most bitter. It will come, though people are unmindful of it; for Allah never breaks a promise.

CHAPTER TWENTY FIVE

The Inventor of Falsehood

It is absolutely vital that we reflect on the words of Allah, revealed in His Scriptures; using His Light to see our way: especially now, at a time when cards are mixed up, when feelings are stupefied, when enthusiasm is dulled; now is the time to return to the great light.

Let's get a guiding light from the words of the Lord.

1. Wrong doing   is   inventing falsehood
"If any, after this, invent a lie and attribute it to Allah, they are indeed unjust wrong-doers." (3:94)

2. Idolatry   is   inventing falsehood
"To set partners with Allah is devising a sin most heinous indeed." (4:48)

3. Disbelief   is   inventing falsehood
"It is the unbelievers who invent lies against Allah; but most of them lack wisdom." (5:103)

4. Failing to believe   is   inventing falsehood
"It is those who do not believe in the Signs of Allah, that forge falsehood: it is they who lie!" (16:105)

5. Rejecting truth   is   inventing falsehood
"And who does more wrong than he who invents a lie against Allah or rejects the Truth when it reaches him? Is there not a home in Hell for those who reject Faith?" (29:68)

6. Lying against Allah   is   inventing falsehood
"Who can be more wicked than one who invents a lie against Allah, or says: 'I have received inspiration,' when he has received none." (6:93)

7. Leading men astray
     without knowledge   is   inventing falsehood
"But who does more wrong than one who invents a lie against Allah to lead astray men without knowledge? For Allah does not guide people who do wrong." (6:144)

8. Rejecting the
     Signs of Allah   is   inventing falsehood
"Who does more wrong than he who invents a lie against Allah or rejects His signs? But verily the wrong-doers shall never prosper." (6:21)

9. Returning to the
     unbelievers' religion,
     failing to dissociate
     oneself from them   is   inventing falsehood.
Shu'aib, peace be upon him is reported in the Qur'an to have said to his people:
"We should indeed invent a lie against Allah, if we returned to you religion after Allah has rescued us therefrom; nor could we by any manner of means return thereto unless it be as the will and plan of Allah, our Lord. Our Lord can reach out to the utmost recesses of things by His knowledge. In Allah is our trust." (7:89)

So, now we have seen who is an inventor of lies, and what is inventing lies; we need to look into the outcomes of inventing lies "By their fruit you will recognize them." (Matthew, 7:16). Here are the outcomes:

1. The wrath of Allah
2. Humiliation in the life of this world
3. Frustration
4. Lacking prosperity

The above list is drawn from several verses of the Qur'an: "Those who took the calf for worship will indeed be overwhelmed with wrath from their Lord, and with humiliation in this life: thus do We recompense those who invent falsehoods." (7:152)

"Say: 'Those who invent a lie against Allah will never prosper.'" (10:69)

Moses, peace be upon him, is reported to have said:

"The forger of lies must suffer frustration." (20:61)

And now that we have learnt in the light of the Almighty's words who is an inventor of lies, and the outcome of inventing lies, we need to look at the events of history. That for one thing; for another, we should look attentively at present events: for we shall here hear the preachers of the Friday prayer inventing lies against Allah, claiming in the meanwhile that if they hit upon the truth when they preach, then they will have a double reward; and if they do an error in what they say, they will still earn one reward: they say that in defiance of the words of Allah, most evident and manifest, as plain as the bright day:

"But who does more wrong than one who invents a lie against Allah, to lead astray men without knowledge?" (6:144)

Actually, what they say in their sermons is not from Allah: the *taghoot*-controlled scholars practice their ignorance, which has grown to be lying and forging falsehood against Allah. It is inspired to them by their devils – Allah is certainly clear from what they utter, as we may learn from the verse just quoted.

It is incumbent on us to announce the truth, and to face that group by challenging the falsehood uttered by their mouths. What they are trying to do is to extinguish the Light of Allah with their mouths – but Allah will complete His Light, no matter how averse the idolaters might be! Those people invent lies against Allah when they enumerate the fundamentals of Islam, though they have no knowledge of the Scriptures of Allah, nor His religion: they are there, sitting in the *taghoot*'s lap, or else conspiring to assassinate the *taghoots*. And they keep oscillating between these two extremes.

Indeed, even if you see evil taking deeper roots and dominating more land, truth is more stable and more powerful. Allah will hurl truth against falsehood and it will knock out its brain, and woe will be to those people for the false things they ascribe to Allah.

CHAPTER TWENTY SIX

The Concept of State and the Concept of Allah's Kingdom

Aristotle is known to be the inspirer of the concept of the modern state. He noticed that the family was the nucleus, and it was the family that begot the state, as a means to ensuring security and survival. By some families linking to other families, extensive families were formed, and from extensive families were established villages; many villages linking together formed the state, and the state later had an authority. The latter determined the kind of policy that served its interests and aims.

A positive approach to the emergence of the state in history takes politics to be the science of social happiness, and takes the function of the state to be ensuring an optimal amount of happiness for its citizens. The actual state of things, however, is otherwise, and history is the best witness in refuting the above representation.

Man is actually being deceived by this:

The sociologists and philosophers assert that it is in man's nature to keep evolving towards perfection; and that evolution cannot take place away from the urban and national society. They add that only a god or an animal can live away from a town. Sociologists claim that the aim of existence is creating a state within a structure that they call civic, and that a state is naturally divided into two nodes, a governor and the governed.

That according to them is the highest destination of man's evolution: for nothing can bring goodness better than a state! But if we undertake to investigate the history of the governor and the government, we shall find that they are the outcome of terrorism: it is so since the governor and the government start with issuing orders, and they enforce those orders through force (terrorism). Later, with passing ages, the obeying of orders becomes a kind of common agreement and contract between the governors and the governed. It is made plausible under such slogan as, 'We the people.' And here lies the distinction between

a. The systems of tyranny, which operate in the world, both at present and those gone by.

In such systems there is always the seed of terrorism: that is imposing by force the theory of the governor and the governed; which is later called a contract and agreement, and it goes into force under the pretext of election: that it is people themselves who elected and determined their own destiny.

b. The system of those who have been graced by Allah; and this is nowhere to be found in the world at present. It works on the principle of:

"No compulsion in religion (i.e. nor in politics): Truth stands out clear from error; whoever rejects evil and believes in Allah has grasped the most trustworthy hand-hold, that never breaks." (The Qur'an, 2:256)

Truth, as you see, is shown in rejecting evil and believing in Allah (that is to dismiss from your heart any affection for the members of your family who work for the *taghoot*: for the latter does not attain rule except through terrorism, though he hides behind the glamour of elections and democracy.

As for 'error' in the above text, it is imposing by force (terrorism) the theory of the governor and the governed – and that is the way all the *taghoots* of the earth came to be rulers: all those that go under striking designations, attended with all the aurora calculated to mislead the multitudes, so that they would not examine the real origin of those figures.

Think of Christ, peace be upon him, who, for building the Kingdom of Allah, started by training the nucleus. Then he dispatched his disciples to teach what they had learned from him. But then, when the trial came, his followers let him down: they betrayed him, abandoned him, and fled. Hence his saying, "My kingdom is not of this world. If it were, my servants would fight and prevent my arrest," (John, 18:36). As for Muhammad, peace be upon him, he was able to establish the Kingdom of Allah, because his followers received him with, "The moon has shone on us. We are bound to thank Allah, with every prayer raised to Allah." And yet, even this kingdom was soon to crumble, when Muslims divided into Sunnis and Shiites: and neither group was able to find the way of that son of Adam who said to his brother, "If you stretch your hand against me, to slay me, it is not for me to stretch my hand against you to slay you: for I do fear Allah, the Lord of the Worlds." (The Qur'an, 5:28)

And so, our Lord makes it plain to us that there are no more than two systems: we either prostrate ourselves to Allah willingly (which is the way of those who win Allah's pleasure) or we prostrate ourselves in spite of us, and that is what happens when one group is an enemy of the other (the governor and the governed). That latter alternative is what is taking place in the world now: people kill each other, and they compete to have atomic weapons. Some forbid others from developing it: and the pretext is: 'I have enough wisdom not to use it, while the other is a terrorist;' that when the term 'terrorist' is more true of former, and that is what one may ascertain by referring to dictionaries. It recalls to mind that a wise man was asked: 'What is the hardest thing in life?' 'It is to know yourself,' he answered.

Authority
As we said, sociologists divide people into two nodes, a governor and the governed. From the concept of authority a governor derives his power to manage the territory that comes under his dominance. Now the sociologists will add that those who are talented to rule tend to rule, while the others have no alternative but to be ruled, for they lack the talent to be rulers.

The social and civic discrimination starts from this, and this is the basis for the inferior attitude towards others, whether adopted by individuals, nations or races. In justifying this concept, Aristotle claimed that the west, the Greeks in his terms, had naturally the traits of courage and superiority that preclude their being enslaved. The Orient, according to this classification, is naturally prone to being enslaved (See John Locke on Civil Rule: My reference is a translation of this book into Arabic by Majed Fakhri, published in Beirut, 1959; page 17)

What Aristotle did was to lay the basis for the Western socio-political thought. He also sowed the seeds of configuring things in dualities:

governor	vs.	governed
master	vs.	slave
king	vs.	subjects
man	vs.	woman

Aristotle mocks at the same time the democratic system which, according to him, is like a home without a master; or like a weak father who has no will to manage the affairs of his own household.

A state for Aristotle is different from a government. The former is a number of citizens who live on the same territory, but territory is not enough for Aristotle to define citizenship: the defining quality of citizenship is the right to participate in legislative and executive affairs. It is a grey representation, that of Aristotle – it is just impossible for the individual to perceive the state of slavery that is applied in the name of citizenship. The other entity, that of government, is defined by Aristotle as a group of people who manage the affairs of the state and overview citizens' affairs. He does classify governments into good and bad ones, but the criteria for that classification are quite variable and unstable. And then Aristotle ranks ruling systems into three categories:

1. A good aristocratic System, in which authority is in the hand of a group that enjoys certain prerogatives. Authority in this system has been taken over by a group after it was in the hand of an individual. A bad aristocratic system is called an oligarchy in Aristotle's representation.

2. A good constitutional system must put the authority in the hands of the majority. Otherwise it is a demagogy in Aristotle's classification.

3. The royal system is good when authority is in the hand of an individual who cares for the public interests and enforces law. A bad royal system is called a dictatorship.

What I have been trying to do is not so much to present Aristotle's theory as to demonstrate the theoretical and methodical bases of the system adopted in the West at a certain stage. The West takes Aristotle's theory about state and society to be the source from which all subsequent thought was a modification rather than a genuine innovation.

All the rationalizations employed by all sorts of rulers, including the dictator, the tyrant, the despot, stem from that social duality put forth by Aristotle, according to which society consists of a governor and the governed.

It is from this polarity that social conflict starts: the governed rebel against the governor and his government, and in consequence of this, streams of blood will be spilled, and all that will be part of man's consciousness and spirit.

Let's suppose for argument's sake that we accepted Aristotle's polarity theory. How should we after that keep silent when it is supposed that a king would take care of the general interests of individuals? Can the great Master Aristotle convince me that politics is the science of social happiness, that the function of a state is to realize happiness for the biggest possible number of citizens?

The primary question is: Is that polarity a predetermined thing? Is it inevitable that in any civic, urban gathering there will be a governor and the governed? It must be evident by now in the present book, and as will be elaborated further on the coming pages, that a society as described by Allah is not divided into a governor and the governed: all are governed within one network defined by Allah. No ruler may enjoy a legislative or an executive authority that gives him a privilege over ordinary individuals. All are members in the Kingdom of Allah, in the state of Allah. Their task, each one of them, is to develop that Kingdom, and no one is to occupy a higher position, if he happens to be a ruler: the sole Ruler is Allah, the Almighty, and man will go on living a life of wretchedness unless and until he discovers the delusion of the duality of society; and until he starts discarding that duality, a duality which discriminates man from the other fellow men. All must come under the one canopy of Allah that has room for all of them. Here is a chart that represents the social system as defined by the Lord:

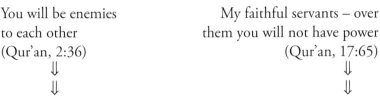

| You will be enemies to each other (Qur'an, 2:36) ⇓ ⇓ This is prostrating oneself in spite of oneself | My faithful servants – over them you will not have power (Qur'an, 17:65) ⇓ ⇓ This is prostrating oneself to Allah willingly |

The above chart summarizes the social system as put forth by Allah.

But the clerics have done so much mischief on the earth that people no longer have confidence, and no longer trust those in authority. However, people do not at the same time know what the alternative should be, or who must be installed instead of the present people. The alternative, in fact, is not a certain person or group: it is realizing the truth ('the truth will make you free,' John, 8:32). Being cognizant of truth, which is the religion of Allah, will release one from the chains of the delusions brought about by the clerics and the politicians. The idea, then, is not to look for a man or a woman or a child, but to look for the system – to search for Allah's system and study it. What the clerics offer, and what they can envision, is straying. Truth is there, all written down: but we need to erase from our memory the myths which have been implanted in men's minds over two thousand years.

The concept of the Kingdom of Allah is quite unlike the state in Aristotle's approach, and quite unlike the modern conception of the state. In the Kingdom of Allah each institution works independently from any other; each functioning by a contract with the people. The Kingdom of Allah is a 'blind' judge, i.e. a judge that has no prejudice in favor of any of the institutions, a perfectly just judge. In the Kingdom of Allah, there is no army: each individual is a soldier in such kingdom. None of the institutions, nor the one who runs it, has any authority to dispatch an army to any war: for the person seated on the throne of the Kingdom of Allah (the caliph), who is there by election, is bound by a contract of referral: it is he who decides about war and peace. There is also the board of the judges of the Kingdom of Allah: they are entrusted with seeking evidence from the words of Allah in the Holy Qur'an to decide whether or not the conditions for fighting are realized. Such conditions should not be set by opinion, guesswork, or by somebody's wish: they are arrived at after sifting the proofs, and the evidence will be nothing but the words of Allah, as recorded in His Scripture.

The army is there for drilling people in the skills of fighting, and nothing else. The chief of institutions is not entitled in the Kingdom of Allah to jail people, or execute them, or torture them. Man's allegiance is not to the state, nor the flag, nor to any such mythical thing: it is solely to Him Who created man, and that is so by a covenant between the Creator of man and man: "Choose no guardian beside Me." (the Qur'an, 17:2)

The management of any of the institutions in the Kingdom of Allah is bound by a written contract with the concerned person: the latter can sue the management at the law court of the Kingdom of Allah, in case it fails to meet the articles of the written contract. There is not, in the Kingdom of Allah, a governor and governed people: he who manages that kingdom is a mere servant who is there not to be served, but to serve: he has been elected by a majority of votes; he is quite conscious of the meaning of turning to Allah; he willingly submits to the ties of that state: he is dedicated since he fully knows that there is no way for him to break free from those ties – in fact each individual in that kingdom is aware of the ties: he is mindful of the ties, and is all the time mindful of Him who controls those ties. Jihad in that kingdom is to announce the truth, in public, should one notice that it is not fulfilled. That Kingdom is divided into two parties: **the first** (Allah and His Messenger) is mentioned in the following verse:

"It is not fitting for a believer, man or woman, when a matter has been decided by Allah and His Messenger, to have any option about their decision: if any one disobeys Allah and His Messenger, he is indeed on a clearly wrong path." (33:36)

The **other party** includes both the administration and the people; and about both the Lord says:

"Who conduct their affairs by mutual consultation." (42:38)
The Kingdom of Allah may not intervene in administration: for it is a contract between an institution and the people. Should either party fail to abide by the contract signed by both parties, and written down at the time of its making, then the plaintiff may submit his case to the independent judiciary authority. This last is divided too into two divisions, a local division and a supreme one. Now this last is entitled to bring the government to count: for in the Kingdom of Allah man is bound twice, as we said earlier; and here you see how the Kingdom can bring the government to task.
In other words, the administration does not rule; and man (who has submitted) is not ruled: there is only a contract between two parties to ensure justice on the earth, everywhere on the earth. It is exactly in the same way as when you go to a bakery to buy your bread: the sales assistant is here not a governor, nor are you governed; and yet, you abide by order when you stand in queue, and you wait for your turn. Once your turn comes you pay for your bread, you are received with a smile: you are served with pleasure because you pay from your precious money for the

service. It is the same with the government in the Kingdom of Allah.

It is not surprising that people do not seem to comprehend when we talk about justice. They have not known Allah's religion; and they can only understand what they see with their eyes, and what their eyes see is the injustice of the *taghoots* of the earth. For instance, it is unjust and a transgression that you sell people a water bottle. No one has the right to sell water: water belongs to all men, and to all animals and plants besides. Men are also entitled to have their water unpolluted; and that is not a favor or a boon offered by somebody. A government or any company is not entitled to sell water or to have possession of water. About that we have these words of the Almighty's:

"And tell them that the water is to be divided between them: each one's right to drink being brought forward by suitable turns." (54:28)

The water company which lays the pipes and provides water has the right to charge people for that; but the people have the right to change that firm should they not be satisfied with its services or its charges. To apply this on earth, all over the globe, is justice: it is definitely not that which is claimed by those who harp on democracy and tyranny.

CHAPTER TWENTY SEVEN

The Waster of Himself

Who is a waster of himself?

To define a waster of himself, we need to look into his recompense, and then we can define him. The Lord describes this type of person as having existed from the moment man descended to this world: He says, as we recite in the Qur'an:

"He said: 'Get you down, both of you – all together, from the Garden, with enmity one to another; but if, as is sure, there come to you guidance from Me, whosoever follows My guidance, will not lose his way, nor fall into misery. But whosoever turns away from My remembrance, verily for him is a life narrowed down, and We shall raise him up blind on the Day of Judgment. He will say: "O my Lord! Why have you raised me up blind, while I had sight before?" Allah will say: "Thus did you, when Our Signs came to you, disregard them: so will you, this day, be disregarded." And thus we recompense him who is a waster of himself beyond bounds and who does not believe in the Signs of his Lord: and the penalty of the Hereafter is far more grievous and more enduring.'" (20:123-127)

By analyzing the above verses we find that the waster of himself brings destruction on himself because of the following reasons:

1. He does not follow the guidance sent down by Allah.
2. He turns away from remembering Allah.
3. He disregards the Signs of Allah.
4. He did not believe in the Signs of his Lord.

And because of all the above, Allah will punish him with the following:
1. A life narrowed down.
2. Raising him up as blind on the Day of Judgment.
3. A grievous penalty in the Hereafter.

The penalty of a waster of himself will be both in this world, and a far more grievous and more enduring penalty in the Hereafter. Let's put this more graphically:

1. The one who follows the guidance of Allah
   $\longrightarrow$ will not lose his way, nor fall into misery

2. The one who turns away from remembering Allah
   $\longrightarrow$ will have a life narrowed down

Now we come to a very important question:

Is Muslims' life narrowed down at present? Are they miserable in this world? Is man still an enemy of man? I leave the answers to the reader.

A waster of himself brings upon himself his own destruction.

Another thing to notice is that wasting oneself is conducive to straying; and about this we may refer to the words of the Almighty:

"And to you there came Joseph in times gone by, with clear Signs, but you did not cease to doubt of the mission for which he had come: at length, when he died, you said: 'Allah will not send any messenger after him.' Thus Allah leaves to stray such as wastes himself and lives in doubt." (40:34)

Allah makes going beyond the bounds laid by Him as a sign of wasting oneself, as we notice in the following verse:

"For you practice your lusts on men in preference to women: you are indeed a people wasting yourselves beyond bounds." (7:81)

CHAPTER TWENTY EIGHT

The Hypocrite

Let's begin with some couplets, relevant to the present topic:

> I have been searching for some religious persons;
> Who are diligent worshippers, but without hypocrisy.
> So I found that while the masses have no intellect,
> To help them perceive arguments, and no light –
> The bright people are quite vain,
> Behaving as prophets sent to men.
> The latter are full of intrigue,
> And the former are too dull to plot.

About the hypocrites, the Almighty Lord tells us several facts:

1. "They are the enemies; so beware of them."(63:4)
2. "The hypocrites are indeed liars." (63:1)
3. "They obstruct men from the Path of Allah." (63:2)
4. "But the hypocrites do not understand." (63:7)
5. "Allah will not forgive them." (63:6)
6. "They believed, then they rejected Faith: so a seal was set on their hearts." (63:3)
7. "You (believers) arouse in their bosoms a fear more intense than even their fear of Allah." (59:13)
8. "You would think they are united, but their hearts are divided." (59:14)

9. "Like the devil, when he says to man, 'Deny Allah': but when man denies Allah, the devil says, 'I am free of you: I do fear Allah, the Lord of the Worlds.'" (59:16)
10. "Those who declare that they believe in the revelations that have come to you and to those before you." (4:60)
11. "Their real wish is to resort together for judgment in their disputes to the *taghoot*." (4:60)

You see how the *taghoot*-controlled scholars claim that America and Israel are the enemy, while the Almighty Allah says that the hypocrites are the enemy. He gives us eleven traits of the hypocrites. And I made a point of listing all the traits to draw the reader's attention to those who go to Mecca and address Allah with the words: "In obedience we come to You;" and then you hear the same people say to the Arab *taghoots*: "In obedience we come to you, O Arab *taghoot*! In obedience! With our lifeblood we defend you, and with our souls!"

Allah has illustrated to His Messenger and to believers what they should do with regard to hypocrites, with such commands as: keep clear of them; do not obey them; disregard their noxious talk; beware of taking them for protectors and friends; be tough to them and do jihad in dealing with them.

Let's quote in conclusion the following words of the Almighty as an additional light on this group:

"The Arabs of the desert are the worst in unbelief and hypocrisy, and most fitted to be in ignorance of the command which Allah has sent down to His Messenger: but Allah is All-Knowing, All-Wise." (9:97)

If you reflect attentively on the above traits, you will find that they are true of those who call themselves 'Muslims'.

CHAPTER TWENTY NINE

The Miserable

It is because Allah cares for men that He warned them of misery, and He pointed out what brings it about – but despite all that we see with our own eyes in how many ways man all over the earth is living in misery.

The misery of toiling and drudgery; misery of loss and straying; misery of anxiety and doubt; misery of pain and destitution: man is too often hungry, thirsty and naked; he is too often massacred or made to sacrifice. All those forms of misery are the result of man's straying on the earth, all the earth. He could, he still can escape that straying and misery in the earth – and misery in the Hereafter is greater – if man but knew!

In Allah's definition, a miserable person is he who does not follow the guidance from Allah; he who follows Satan, for the latter will lead him out of Allah's blessing to the wretchedness of life on earth. At the same time, Allah promises man that, if he follows His guidance, he will neither stray nor be miserable.

Allah warns man against his enemy, who will cause him misery should he follow him. That is what we have in the following words of the Almighty's:

"Verily, this is an enemy to you and your wife: so let him not get you both out of the Garden, so that you are landed in misery." (20:117)

To make man always remember the enemy, the Lord used the pronoun 'this'; and He pointed out that following that enemy will land one into misery. But unfortunately man has forgotten the words of Allah, and so he was, and still is, in misery. The Qur'an was sent down by Allah so that man gets over his misery: through learning Allah's Scriptures man will end his misery on this earth, and will later be in eternal ecstasy. That is what we learn from these words of the Almighty, addressed to His Messenger:

"We have not sent down the Qur'an to you to be in misery." (20:2)

Although Allah has warned man against his enemy, or rather enemies, He has not commanded him to kill his enemy to enjoy life. He commands him to behave in the way of Abraham, peace be upon him: he asked his people not to follow Satan, and when his father said, as the Qur'an reports:

"O Abraham, if you do not forbear, I will indeed stone you: so get away from me for a good long while!" Abraham's answer was: "Peace be on you: I will pray to my Lord for your forgiveness: for He is to me Most Gracious. And I will turn away from you all and from those whom you invoke besides Allah: I will call on my Lord: perhaps, by my prayer to my Lord, I shall be not miserable." (19:47-48)

So that was Abraham's manner of dealing with the enemies of Allah: by turning away from them, and by praying for them. And what was his reward from Allah? Again we turn to the Qur'an:

"When he had turned away from them and from those whom they worshipped besides Allah, We bestowed on him Isaac and Jacob, and each one of them We made a prophet. And We bestowed of Our Mercy on them, and We granted them lofty honor on the tongue of truth." (19:49-50)

That was the reward for Abraham's responding to the command of Allah and shunning the *taghoot*: Allah decreed that Abraham's progeny should be a series of prophets that led mankind.

As we said above, according to people, the world consists of rulers and the ruled, oppressor and the oppressed, strong and weak.

But in the system of Allah, there are in the world three types: an arrogant person, an oppressed person, and a prostrating person. Both the arrogant and the oppressed are roaming aimlessly in the earth, and they will end up in misery. As for the prostrating person, he is the one who has dissociated himself; he is well guided and he is dedicated to obeying the commands and shunning the prohibitions of Allah. Dedication and dissociation are the two safeguards which will withstand any aggression leveled by the powers of evil and tyranny: they are sure to protect the person who has them from any harm. The pointless arrogance of tyrants enhances faith and trust in the heart of a dedicated believer: he will remember that it is only his Lord that is to be feared; he will remember the ultimate end of tyranny, denial and rejection; and he will realize that peace is for the one who follows good guidance, while penalty is for the one who rejects truth and turns away from his Lord. Once all that is recalled to his mind, the dedicated believer will think of the vast existence; he will imagine the creative potential of a devoted nucleus, a prostrating believer; he will feel the vibrant life endowed by the Almighty to existence; and he will feel great tranquility, that he is safe from straying and misery: for these two are the outcome of disobedience. Life, the nucleus will reason within his mind: miserable indeed are the straying: their life is no more than toil, drudgery, anxiety, doubt, loss, agony, hunger and nakedness; while he is blessed with a life of guidance on the straight path; a life of endeavoring to establish the Kingdom of Allah – a Kingdom where the arrogant and the oppressed are not to be encountered: for in that place there is room only for one who clings to the five conditions of prostration.

CHAPTER THIRTY

The Misguided

Misguidance as used in the Qur'an is from Allah: It is Allah who misguided Satan, for the latter addressed Allah with the words, "Because You have misguided me, my Lord ..." (7:16) Noah also said to his people, as reported in the Qur'an: "If it be that Allah wills to misguide you: He is your Lord! and to Him will you return." (11:34)

Misguidance is from Allah, but it is the penalty for a crime committed by man. See for instance, "Thus Adam disobeyed his Lord, and let himself be misguided." (20:121)

Let's recite more about misguidance in the Qur'an:

"Relate to them the story of the man to whom We sent Our Signs, but he passed them by: so Satan followed him up, and he was misguided. If it had been Our Will, We should have elevated him with Our Signs; but he inclined to the earth, and followed his own vain desires. His similitude is that of a dog: if you attack him, he lolls out his tongue, or if you leave him alone, he still lolls out his tongue. That is the similitude of those who reject Our Signs, so relate the story; perchance they may reflect. Evil as an example are people who reject Our Signs and wrong their own souls." (7:175-177)

When man disregards the Signs of his Lord his penalty will be misguidance; that is again what we may learn from the Qur'an:

"Those who behave arrogantly on the earth in defiance of right – I will turn them away from My Signs: Even if they see all the Signs, they will not believe in them; and if they see the way of right conduct, they will not adopt it as the way; but if they see the way of misguidance, that is the way they will adopt. For they have rejected Our Signs, and failed to take warning from them." (7:146)

As you see, the True Lord has pointed out what is misguidance, what steps lead up to it, and what its causes are.

Disobeying any command of Allah's is the first step on the way to misguidance. But Allah describes more landmarks on the way to misguidance. He says elsewhere:

"But after them there followed a posterity who missed prayers and followed after lust; soon, then, they will fall into misguidance." (19:59)

When man loses communion with Allah, and when he follows after his desires and lusts, disregarding the limits ordained by Allah – he will have taken the first step on the way to misguidance. Those steps have three sources:

1. Source one: man's self ⇒⇒ 'followed after their lusts' (disobedience)
2. Source two: the devil ⇒⇒ Failing to be sincere to Allah (as in the verses: "Iblis said: 'O my Lord! because You have misguided me, I will make wrong fair-seeming to them on the earth, and I will misguide them all – except Your servants among them, sincere and purified.'" (15:39-40) Satan's misguidance will happen to every man and every group except for **'Allah's sincere and purified servants'**,

for sincerity protects them as if they had a high wall that
obstructs Satan's infiltration.

3. Source three: The assumed associates of Allah ⇒⇒ that
is, when a man misguides another man, instigating him
to disobey Allah and follow after his lusts. That situation
is described by the Almighty in the following words:
"The Day Allah will call to them, and say: 'Where are My
partners whom you imagined to be such?' Those against
whom the charge will be proved, will say: 'Our Lord!
These are the ones whom we misguided: we misguided
as we were misguided ourselves: we free ourselves from
them in Your presence: it was not us they worshipped.'"
(28:63-64)

A man that abandons Allah and follows another man, a tyrant
or whoever else, that other man will disavow him on the Last Day:
when Allah calls to them: those others will say **'It was not us they
worshipped.'** Allah is reminding us that both the one who does
misguidance and the misguided will receive the same recompense:
that is what one learns from the following words of the Almighty's:
"And they will turn to one another, and question one another. They
will say: 'It was you who used to come to us from the right hand
(of power and authority)!' They will reply: 'Nay, you yourselves
had no faith! Nor had we any authority over you. Nay, it was you
who were a people in obstinate rebellion! So now has been proved
true, against us, the Word of the Lord that we shall indeed have to
taste the punishment of our sins. We did misguide you: for truly,
we were ourselves misguided.' Truly, that Day, they will all share in
the penalty. Verily that is how We shall deal with the sinners. For
they, when they were told that there is no god except Allah, would
puff themselves up with pride." (37:27-35)

So they are in two types, as described by the Lord, some
arrogant, and some oppressed.

CHAPTER THIRTY ONE

The Law of 'If and Only If'

Christ, peace be on him, strove to teach men to dispose of regional pride, national pride, and racism: he urged them to remember they belonged to one human race; he exhorted them to be cooperative and merciful to each other; as they belonged to One God, who placed them on this earth, and set for them the way to lead. It was clear to Christ that these facts were certain to ensure that mankind may not be in misery.

Hence, we find Christ, peace be upon him, focusing on one target: to guide men to the right way. You find him say: "Come unto me, all ye that labor and are heavy laden, and I will give you rest. Take my yoke upon you, and learn of me... For my yoke is easy, and my burden is light." (Matthew, 11:28-30) Jesus knew well the target of human life, and that is the erection of the Kingdom of Allah on earth: a Kingdom where man will live without suffering hunger or thirst, without being naked or being exposed to the hot sun. Man hopes to have a happy life on earth. It is a place where the environment is protected from pollution; a place where justice is maintained; a place where arrogance that leads to more sin is banished, and so is a mind closed up to all comprehension. It is a place where goodness reigns, and evil is banished and eliminated.

It is a Kingdom which is ruled by laws that are called by the Almighty: 'the ways of life before you,' (3:137). The establishment of that Kingdom is based on principles and sciences derived from 'the Ways of Allah', in harmony with the straight way, the way of those on whom Allah has bestowed His Grace, those whose portion is not His wrath, and who do not go astray. That is the right approach to understanding the ways of Allah. Once that is realized, we will have the remedy for man, the nucleus, from any mishaps he may encounter in his life. We may be sure then that he can be free from the complexes and psychological disorders that are usually contracted from the community in which a human happens to live. There will also be a remedy, by learning the ways of Allah and adhering to the straight way, to social malaise, for no society in the present world is free from that.

Abraham, peace be upon him, was clear about all the grace that is obtained in this way, as we may see in his saying, as quoted in the Qur'an:

"[He] Who created me, and it is He who guides me; Who gives me food and drink, and when I am ill, it is He who cures me; Who will cause me to die, and then to live again; and Who, I hope, will forgive me my faults on the Day of Judgment." (26:78-82)

Directly from the Lord we have:
"And those saved from the covetousness of their own souls – they are the ones that achieve prosperity." (64:16)

As you see to be saved from stinginess will ensure prosperity in this world and the Hereafter – and yet one should have the prosperity as his target, in which case both the prosperity of this world and the Hereafter will be won. While, if one seeks prosperity in this world, he will lose both. That was crystal clear to Jesus when he said:

"But seek ye first the kingdom of God, and his righteousness; and these things shall be added unto you." (Matthew, 6:33)

Allah, Who created man, is a Doer of all that He wills to do; and He willed to create man who also can do all he wills: that will is the distinguishing trait: you either have the will to realize, build and develop that kingdom; or you do not realize it, building nothing and developing nothing. In the latter case man will be just a beast, even though he has the form of a human: he will fall down, far down; and he will toil, feel hunger and thirst, and be scorched with the sun, exactly as we see him now.

When man descends to that abyss, it will be true of him what Isaiah said, as reported in the Bible,

"I have nourished and brought up children, and they have rebelled against me. The ox knoweth his owner, and the ass his master's crib: but Israel doth not know, my people doth not consider." (Isaiah, 1:2-3)

Consider especially the expression 'rebelled against me', for we are discussing people who do what they do thinking meanwhile that they are complying with the religion of Allah: but indeed how can fish live outside water!

What delays the erection of the Kingdom of Allah is the absence of the concept of the Signs of Allah and the concept of the straight way and obedience; to hope to see the kingdom established without these two is like a fish hoping to live without water. And here comes the law of 'if and only if': for this law about what is required for establishing the kingdom is a closed circle: you can add nothing to it, nor can you detract anything. You may note in the Qur'an how Allah puts, in the conditional structures, man's act before the Lord's act, so that it is categorically established that in case anything goes wrong, the responsibility is completely upon man: it is he who Allah appointed viceroy on the earth. Should man or society face any predicament, it is the result of what man did or failed to do; it may be the result of his not comprehending one or more of Allah's laws pertaining to man or society. Man has been give the will prior to this struggle of his; and will, as we said above, is the critical element in this connection.

It may be noticed how manifest this fact was to Christ in the following quotation:

"As the Father knoweth me, even so know I the Father: and I lay down my life for the sheep. And other sheep I have, which are not of this fold; them also I must bring, and they shall hear my voice; and there shall be one fold, and one shepherd. Therefore doth my Father love me, because I lay down my life, that I might take it again. No man taketh it from me, but I lay it down of myself. I have power to lay it down, and I have power to take it again. This commandment have I received of my Father." (John, 10:15-18)

Think well about the Qur'an: it does not produce its fruit; and that is because those who bear it do not understand what they hold. If you are wondering what the evidence of the above claim is, my answer is:

Ask a random hundred Muslims who claim to know their religion the following question:

What topics are handled by the Holy Qur'an, and how many are they?

From the hundred individuals you will get a hundred answers, each different from the others. They will not have the same opinion simply because they do not know the Holy Qur'an, and are not aware of the topics it discusses. The same result would be obtained if one were to ask the children of Israel, and so in the case of those who claim to be followers of Christ. Christ was right in addressing such people with the words,

"Ye fools and blind." (Matthew, 23:17)
Or he sometimes said,
"If the blind lead the blind, both shall fall into the ditch."
(Matthew, 15:14)

Now if you were to take any other book, a book in physics, chemistry, math, biology, or geology and ask those who read such sciences what the topics of the book they have read are, there would be no disagreement at all. So what makes people agree about these books and disagree about the former one? Is it that everyone is wrong? Or is one right and the rest are wrong? It cannot be that they are all right when they disagree so sharply: it is simply something that a sound mind does not accept. If the mind is not sound, well – in that case the same figure can be a cube and a sphere at the same time!

The sciences that are in the Holy Qur'an, or in the sayings of Christ, peace be upon him, prepare man and orient him; they release his mind from the ignorance he live in, so that the horizons of the universe are unfolded before his eyes. He will have the key to entering a closed world, which may not be entered without sincerity and obedience. That is what we may understand from the following words of the Almighty:

"They say: 'Our hearts are under veils, concealed from that to which you invite us, and in our ears is a deafness, and between us and you is a screen: so you do what you will; for us, we shall do what we will!" (41:5)

As for Christ, peace be upon him, he put it in the following words, in response to a question put forth by his disciples about the reason he uses parables in teaching them: "Because it is given unto you to know the mysteries of the kingdom of heaven, but to them it is not given. For whosoever hath, to him shall be given, and he shall have more abundance: but whosoever hath not, from him shall be taken away even that he hath." (Matthew, 13:11-12)

As for guidance and straying, he pointed out that they come according to a law: he said:
"No man can come unto me, except it were given unto him of my Father." (John, 6:65)

See how similar the above is to the following words in the Holy Qur'an:
"No soul can believe, except by the Will of Allah." (10:100)

It transpires that it is Allah who guides and it is He who misguides. However, guidance and misguidance are cause-related, both subject to a law, as we said above. Allah will not guide a liar who is wont to disbelieve; He misguides the miscreant.

What we have, then, is a free man who chooses to submit his own will to replace it with the Supreme Will, the Will of the One Who created the universe. That again is clear in the words of Christ, who surrendered his will, and said:
"Thy kingdom come. Thy will be done in earth, as it is in heaven." (Matthew, 6:10)

He realized that the kingdom of Allah would not come unless man abandoned his own will. Of course Christ, peace be on him, did not establish the kingdom of Allah, because all his followers betrayed him. And he told them about that betrayal, that they all would betray him; that is what the Bible tells us:
"But the scriptures must be fulfilled. And they all forsook him, and fled." (Mark, 14:49-50)

Christ used to say,
"He that is not with me is against me." (Matthew, 12:30)

It was clear to Christ that the betrayal would take place; that his followers would not protect him, or defend him, by defying those of the children of Israel who denied him. Therefore he said: "My kingdom is not of this world: if my kingdom were of this world, then would my servants fight, that I should not be delivered to the Jews: but now is my kingdom not from hence." (John, 18:36)

The same story is also told in the Qur'an:
"When Jesus found unbelief on their part, he said: 'Who will be my helpers to the work of Allah?' Said the Disciples: 'We are Allah's helpers: we believe in Allah, and you bear witness that we are Muslims. Our Lord! we believe in what You have revealed, and we follow the Messenger; then write us down among those who bear witness.' And the unbelievers plotted and planned, and Allah too planned, and the best of planners is Allah." (4:52-54)

And so, the corpse disappeared. A corpse does not vanish from earth. It originated from the earth, and to the earth it returns. I did describe in my previous book, *Search for Truth*, where the corpse disappeared, and I provided all the proofs related to that. But how can one explain to those who do not study the Holy Qur'an and the sayings of Christ, peace be on him? It is not possible to make the embryo visualize an elephant before it comes out into the world.

The point here is that nothing that afflicts an individual or society but is the result of the individual's or society's deeds or thoughts: it may be the result of man's not perceiving one or more of Allah's laws concerning individuals or groups. Duties are two types: personal and collective; the former is incumbent on the individual personally, and the latter is incumbent on the group, so that once it is fulfilled by some of them, the rest are not bound to do it. This helps us understand Divine Justice, for the outcome of man is always linked to something that is within his capacity. Let me elaborate this point by citing some verses of the Qur'an in which Allah places man's deed ahead of His own deed.

"Allah will never change the conditions of a people until they change what is in their own souls." (13:11)

The act of changing (changing what is in the heart, like allegiance to the *taghoot*, hypocrisy, or any other sin) must first be attended to; not at the level of one individual, but at the level of the society. Unless such change takes place, no change in the welfare of the people will happen. There are some who resort to violence in the hope of effecting a change in this way; and once man has entered the vicious circle of violence, there seems to be no way out of it. The ignorant imagine that to possess weapons is an invincible fortress, and so they go about devising more deadly weapons and more cunning spying, and so on.

The fact is that a *taghoot* is there by the will of Allah; that victory is in the hand of Allah and no one else. That is why we read in the Qur'an:

"Victory comes only from Allah, the Mighty, the Wise." (3:126)

So what if Allah does not grant us victory? It means that there is something we do not understand about failure; and it is our duty to review and study where lies our shortcoming. What we find in the Qur'an is this:

If you aid the cause of Allah ⇒⇒ He will aid you, and plant your feet firmly (47:7)

That man stands for the word of Allah and endeavors to see it rise is a prerequisite of Allah's granting victory to the believer, placing him as viceroy, and promoting his affairs. When victory does not come from Allah, it definitely means that man has not aided the cause of Allah. That is to say, man has not done his best to ensure that the word of Allah is foremost in the world, that it dominates affairs on earth.

Also about the graces Allah grants man, Allah links those graces to man's conduct: He says that He never withdraws those graces unless people change that which is inside their souls. Every time man lets some of the goodness in his heart decrease, Allah withdraws a proportionate amount of His grace; and that can end up in man not having any of Allah's grace, and then he lives in misery. People often are nostalgic about bygone days: they say, 'every day seems to be worse than the day before it.' But those changes are cause-related. See some 'if and only if' laws:

If truth comes $\Rightarrow\Rightarrow$ falsehood will vanish.
Enter the gate prostrate $\Rightarrow\Rightarrow$ and We forgive you your sins.
If you but eschew the most heinous of the things which you are forbidden to do $\Rightarrow\Rightarrow$ We shall remit you of your evil deeds.
When you eliminate from your heart any affection for those who have enmity for Allah $\Rightarrow\Rightarrow$ Allah will write faith upon your heart.
If you do not get over your allegiance to the *taghoot* $\Rightarrow\Rightarrow$ Allah will not remove the *taghoot* from subduing you.
If you do not follow the way of guidance $\Rightarrow\Rightarrow$ those who are misguided will cause you harm.
If you follow guidance $\Rightarrow\Rightarrow$ the misguided cannot harm you.
If man rebels against what he is commanded to do $\Rightarrow\Rightarrow$ Allah will misguide him.
If man is an unbeliever and liar $\Rightarrow\Rightarrow$ Allah will not guide him to the right way.
If anyone's sight is dim to the remembrance of the Beneficent $\Rightarrow\Rightarrow$ We appoint for him a devil, to be an intimate companion to him.
If you are a false, sinful one $\Rightarrow\Rightarrow$ the devil will descend upon you.
If you follow the guidance from Allah $\Rightarrow\Rightarrow$ there is no fear for you.

If you turn away from remembering Allah ⇒⇒ Your life will be narrowed-down and you will be resurrected blind on the Day of Judgment.

When a glamour from the devil troubles those who are pious ⇒⇒ they remember Allah's guidance and behold them seers.

When Allah is mentioned ⇒⇒ the hearts of believers feel fear.

When the revelations of Allah are recited to the believers ⇒⇒ their faith increases.

If you repeat (the crime) ⇒⇒ We repeat (the punishment).

If you fear Allah ⇒⇒ He will forgive you your sins.

Tell those who disbelieve, if they cease (to persecute the believers) ⇒⇒ their past sins will be forgiven them.

But if they return (to their ways) ⇒⇒ the example of those before them has already been given.

What we have in the above laws is that what will bring about the first step in effecting a change is man's deeds: for Allah's deed only follows man's deed. The more man heeds and obeys, the more he is guided and his way is bright with illumination. See for example the following verse from the Qur'an:

"Those who listen to what is said, and follow the best of it: those are the ones whom Allah has guided, and those are the ones endued with understanding." (39:18)

See also the following from Christ, and see how well he realized the above process:

"Because it is given unto you to know the mysteries of the kingdom of heaven, but to them it is not given. For whosoever hath, to him shall be given, and he shall have more abundance: but whosoever hath not, from him shall be taken away even that he hath." (Matthew, 13:11-12)

It is absolutely vital that one perceives this system, and how it works – for it is the only way for the human mind. Any efforts spent in following some other way are lost efforts, and they will go west, without producing any fruit. And it may be further said, that to see that way, there is a definite approach. It is going astray to try to guess and reason for oneself. You must come to terms with the system itself and work in accordance with it: not to do so, will prevent one from seeing his way.

In other words, the Qur'an is self-explanatory: you only need to search through it, and leave behind your suspicions and others' suspicions. As for the sayings of Jesus in the Holy Bible, they comprise the proper meaning of the Holy Qur'an; they are exactly like looking in a mirror. So both the Holy Qur'an and the sayings of Christ are a cure and mercy for mankind; they are the remedy for the diseases we see on earth, everywhere on earth. Injustice comes from man; and to perceive it, put it right, and have patience to see it put it right – that is the first step in establishing the Kingdom of Allah.

Here is some useful discussion of this topic from page 12 of *al-Adab al-Sagheer*, by Ibn Al-Muqffa':

"Let it be known that each creature has needs, that for every need there is an end, and for attaining that end there is a proper way. Now, people's end, what they need, is having a good life in this world and a good life in the Hereafter. The way to attaining that aim is to have a sound mind. You know that someone has a sound mind if you find him judge things by the outcome they lead to. Some people have the patience to work for long-term gratifications, and some do not. So it is common among all human beings to love that which is advantageous to them and detest that which is harmful to them. The difference between people is in patience, the amount of enduring the hardships they will encounter in attaining that which is good for them."

What Muslims now say is that what has befallen us is the result of the weakness and treachery of our *taghoots*; or it is brought about by America or by Israel. That when Allah has succinctly made it plain to us, that any calamity that befalls us is caused by our own selves, and it only happens by the will of Allah.

That is why you find Muslims talk and talk, going through endless disputations that are in vain. The truth, however, stands out as plain as the day.

CHAPTER THIRTY TWO

False Religion and the Defects of Thinking

We have gone rather faster than we had planned. It was said before that religion as it is practiced at present is alien to the true religion, that both the *taghoot* and the clerics have made of religion opium that they use to stupefy people. To drive this idea home, we need to support it with some illustration and evidence, although I fully perceive that I will not be able to do justice to this topic: an issue of this complexity will not be fully appreciated throuth one book; add to this that I have had here to take up other matters. However, we shall have to bring to light and to support the truth, so that foam may pass out as scum to the banks, while that which is of use to people remains in the earth – therefore I say:

Allah did not reveal one religion to the Jews, another to the Arabs, and a third to the followers of Christ. For evidence you may look at the following words of the Almighty, which He addresses to all humankind:
"O you people! Adore your Guardian-Lord, Who created you and those who came before you, that you may have the chance to ward off evil." (2:21)

Or you may look at this other verse:
"Pilgrimage thereto [to Mecca] is a duty men owe to Allah – those who can afford the journey." (3:97)

As you see, it is a duty on men in general, not on Muslims alone. Muslims' worship in Mecca in no more at present than whistling and hand-clapping; and they will taste pain for their disbelief. Such delusions as are rampant in the world today, about separate Islam, Christianity and Judaism, are distortions that have nothing to do with Allah's true religion. Allah's religion is purely and absolutely unitary; it is distinct from any other system, for it comprises a way of life and an integrated system, most accurately and in all its details. Since there is no life or existence in this world without Him Who has created, and further given order and proportion; Who brings out the green luscious pasture – He has ordained that those who fear Allah will remember Him, and will have their due reward.

This is a decisive point about faith – and a decisive point in behavior and life: for he who is in communion with the Creator, who refers to Him for his life, for his system, knowledge, and feelings, must be dissimilar to the one who acts upon vague, hazy and contradictory fancies. The latter does not find in his soul a basis for a Creator who is present in life, and Who directs his steps. What people follow and hold to – whether they are false national ties, straying religious group, or *taghoot*-controlled political parties – can never realize unity among themselves, no matter how many scientific sorcery or alluring national claims are used for the purpose. The fact is that earth, the whole of the earth, is man's homeland: the real source of strength is the Creator. It is on Him that we may rely for law, order, economics, social life, manners, or morality; all else are defective and false fancies. There will be no unity unless the source of direction is one, the destination of direction is united; unless the deity we respond to, obey and worship, with full conviction and conception, is One.

If we examine the reality of this religion we find that it is a pact, a covenant; it is an application of the conditions of prostration, after eschewing the most heinous things which the Creator has forbidden us.

See for instance the pact and covenant Allah made with Noah, peace be on him, as reported in the Bible:
"And God spake unto Noah, and to his sons with him, saying, 'And I, behold, I establish my covenant with you, and with your seed after you.'" (Genesis, 9:8-9)

Similarly, the Bible reports about the covenant and pact with Abraham, peace be on him:
"As for me, behold, my covenant is with thee, and thou shalt be a father of many nations. Neither shall thy name any more be called Abram, but thy name shall be Abraham; for a father of many nations have I made thee. And I will make thee exceeding fruitful, and I will make nations of thee, and kings shall come out of thee. And I sill establish my covenant between me and thee and thy seed after thee in their generations for an everlasting covenant, to be a God unto thee, and to thy seed after thee." (Genesis, 17:4-7)

The same covenant is described in the Qur'an in the following words:
"He said: 'I will make you a leader to the nations.' He pleaded: 'And also leaders from my offspring!' He answered: 'But my promise is not within the reach of evil-doers. Remember We made the House a place of assembly for men and a place of safety; and you take the Station of Abraham as a place of prayer; and we covenanted with Abraham and Isma'il, that they should sanctify My House for those who compass it round, or use it as a retreat, or bow, or prostrate themselves therein in prayer." (2:124-125)

And then, what Christ, peace be upon him, said, as in the Bible:

"It is written, Thou shalt worship the Lord thy God, and him only shalt thour serve." (Matthew, 4:10) is expressed like this in the Qur'an:

"Do not take other than Me as disposer of your affairs." (17:2)

Back to Moses, we find him covey the words of his Lord like, as reported in the Bible:

"If ye walk in my statutes, and keep my commandments, and do therein; then I will give you rain in due season, … And I will give peace in the land, and ye shall lie down, and none shall make you afraid." (Leviticus, 26:3-6)

All the above examples serve to show the unity of religion; but it was the deviations which came about as a result of people's inclinations and intellectual and political trends that enabled certain groups to have dominance over others. As a result, the religion of Allah was abandoned, and men followed the traditions imposed by other men. All that was in the mind of Christ when he said:

"For laying aside the commandment of God, ye hold the traditions of men." (Mark, 7:8)

He well knew how some men were evil, and how they may lead astray other men:

"Beware ye of the leaven of the Pharisees, which is hypocrisy." (Luke, 12:1)

"But Jesus did not commit himself unto them, because he knew all men." (John, 2:24)

We have then support enough to expose those who have abandoned the commandments of the Almighty Lord – which are the fundamentals of prostration – and followed instead their interpretations and fancies, seeking discord, and searching for hidden meaning. They turned their backs to the unitary religion, which had gone on from messenger to messenger of Allah, and from prophet to prophet, all united with the covenant that Allah established between Him and His prophets. Let's read about that in the Qur'an:

"And remember We took from the prophets their Covenant: as We did from you: from Noah, Abraham, Moses and Jesus the son of Mary: we took from them a solemn Covenant: that Allah may question the custodians of truth, concerning the truth they were charged with: and He has prepared for the unbelievers a grievous penalty." (33:7-8)

The Covenant mentioned in the above verse is given in full elsewhere: let's read its text:

"Behold! Allah took the Covenant of the prophets, saying: 'I give you a Book and wisdom; then comes to you a Messenger, confirming what is with you; you believe in him and render him help.' Allah said: 'Do you agree, and take this My Covenant as binding on you?' They said: 'We agree.' He said: 'Then bear witness, and I am with you among the witnesses.' If any turn back after this, they are perverted transgressors." (3:81-82)

Each prophet inherited the Books Allah had revealed before him, and that is what we read about in the Bible:

"The law and the prophets were until John." (Luke, 16:16)

And then Jesus came and told them he was the inheritor of that legacy, that "All that belongs to the Father is mine," (John, 16:15) that anyone who fails to believe would stay in his sin. And he added:

"The Father loveth the Son, and hath given all things into his hand. He that believeth on the Son hath everlasting life: and he that believeth not the Son shall not see life; but the wrath of God abideth on him." (John, 3:35-36)

He told them about one that comes after him, and added, "He will bring glory to me by taking what is mine and making it known to you." (John, 16:14) That again is saying that the Scriptures revealed by Allah to His prophets, and had been inherited by Jesus, were again revealed to Muhammad, peace be on him. But men are unheeding, and they do not perceive what is in the Holy Qur'an. They should look intently at verses like this:

"Say: 'Bring your convincing proof: this is the Message of those before me.' But most of them do not know the truth, and so turn away." (21:24)

It is obviously two distinct things that one has to believe in, but Muslims think them one. See the following verse, too:

"The unbelievers say: 'We shall not believe in this scripture nor in any that came before it.'" (34:31)

So, we know what the Qur'an is; but what is that which came before it?

If you look well at this, you will find the Scriptures of Allah contained in the Holy Qur'an, and each denoting the time it had been revealed, and to whom it had been revealed. Allah had undertaken to preserve His Scriptures, then He revealed them again. About that He said in the Qur'an:

"We have, without doubt, sent down the Message, and We will assuredly guard it." (15:9)

Here is an interesting piece of evidence. Read the following verse carefully; it is about John, peace be upon him: the Lord says:

"So peace on him the day he was born, the day he dies, and the day he will be raised up to life again." (19:15)

Pay good attention to the verb: 'was born'. It is a verb in the past tense; something that has already happened.

Now think about the verb: 'dies'. It is a verb in the present, denoting an event that will happen later on, something in the future.

From this reasoning we conclude that when this chapter was revealed, John, peace be on him, had been born, but was still alive. If this chapter were revealed at the time of the Messenger, and if the chapter belonged to him, the above structure would have been: "So peace on him the day he was born, the day he died, and the day he will be raised up to life again." Both the first verb and the second would have been in the past.

Now the first verb is in the past, and the second in the present, because the relevant Scripture is addressed to Zachariah, peace be upon him, which is clear in the context. When that Scripture was revealed, John was alive: he had been born, but had not yet died. Therefore, when the Lord says: "We have, without doubt, sent down the Message, and We will assuredly guard it;" (15:9), he has actually guarded the Message, exactly as He had revealed it the first time. And then the Scripture was revealed again to the Messenger, which is indicated for those who reflect well: Our Great Lord does always say the truth. It will help to recite some more verses:

"Is then one who knows that that which has been revealed to you from you Lord is the truth, like one who is blind? It is those who are endued with understanding that receive admonition; those who fulfill the Covenant of Allah and do not fail in their plighted word; those who join together those things which Allah has commanded to be joined, hold their Lord in awe, and fear the terrible reckoning; those who patiently persevere, seeking the countenance of their Lord; establish regular prayers; spend, out of the gift We have bestowed for their sustenance, secretly and openly, and turn off evil with good: for such there is the final attainment of the Eternal Home – Gardens of perpetual bliss: they shall enter there, as well as the righteous among their fathers, their spouses, and their offspring: and the angels center unto them from every gate with the salutation: 'Peace unto you for that you persevered in patience! Now how excellent is the final Home!' But those who break the Covenant of Allah, after having plighted their word thereto, and cut asunder those things which Allah has commanded to be joined, and work mischief in the land; on them is the curse; for them is the terrible Home!" (13:19-25)

Therefore you find Jesus, peace be on him warning people that if they did not believe in him they would be living in sin, while if they came to him they would have life. He said:

"Search the scriptures; for in them ye think ye have eternal life; and they are they which testify of me. And ye will not come to me, that ye might have life." (John, 5:39-40)

He said again and again that there was no way to the father except through him, Christ; that he was the only way to God (John, 14:6). And he said:

"I said therefore unto you, that ye shall die in your sins: for if ye believe not that I am he, ye shall die in your sins." (John, 8:24)

The sin that Christ is talking about here is that of cutting off one prophet from another, in defiance of Allah's Covenant to the prophets. He kept repeating and explaining, but nobody understood, and they kept asking him who he was. When he said, "he that sent me is true; and I speak to the world those things which I have heard of him; they understood not that he spake to them of the father." (John, 8:26-27)

Listen to him saying: "I am the way, the truth, and the life: no man cometh unto the Father, but by me." (John, 14:6)

And so, when Messenger Muhammad, peace be upon him, came, the Covenant of the prophets was revealed, and so those who did not believe in Christ were in sin. That is plainly stated in the words of Christ, peace be on him:

"And when he is come, he will reprove the world of sin, and of righteousness, and of judgment: of sin, because they believe not on me." (John, 16:8-9)

That is repeated in the Qur'an in relation to the Covenant of the prophets, that those who cut off what Allah ordained to be continuous are losers.

Muslims fell in the same mistake, for joining things and cutting them off are to them the relations with family members. But if that were true, as Muslims believe, how was it that Abraham severed relations with his father and deserted him? How was it that Muhammad severed relations with his uncle Abu Lahab? How was it that Moses severed relations with the Children of Israel? Should it be as Muslims understand cutting off, then all the prophets of Allah would be in Hell. But Muslim are not aware of contradicting themselves: they indeed do not comprehend, nor perceive: joining things and cutting them off pertain to the Covenant of prophets, when the Lord told them that a messenger would come to them, confirming what they had; and commanded them to believe in him and help him (3:81). It is this, the chain of prophets and messengers: to believe in them all is joining things, and not to believe is cutting off. Hence what we read in the Bible,

"The law and the prophets were until John." (Luke, 16:16)

Therefore you find John, peace be upon him, ask, "Art thou he that should come, or do we look for another?" (Matthew, 11:3) Then Christ's answer was that he was light, and he gave him signs to realize who he was: that the blind saw, the deaf heard, and the dead rose (Matthew, 11:5) John the Baptist definitely understood the significance of the signs, but the others did not.

And Jesus said further,
"Yet a little while is the light with you. Walk while ye have the light, lest darkness come upon you: for he that walketh in darkness knoweth not whither he goeth. While ye have light, believe in the light, that ye may be the children of light." (John, 12:35-36)

If you need more evidence, let me give you another example. In the Qur'an we recite:
"Say: 'O men! I am sent to you all;'"
Notice the word 'I'. Who is talking here? Let's read later in the same verse:
"So believe in Allah and His Messenger, the unlettered Prophet … follow him." (7:158)
So the first pronoun is 'I' ⇒⇒ "Say: 'O men! I am sent to you all;"
The second pronoun is in the third person ⇒⇒ "follow him".

Obviously, the verse tells about two different persons. Now we do know that 'him' refers to the 'unlettered prophet' Muhammad – indeed everybody knows he is the unlettered prophet. So who does the first pronoun 'I' denote?

By reviewing the chapter we find that the Almighty points out there how the sinners are punished. In this connection, He mentions an example in this chapter that was mentioned by Christ, peace be upon him. We read in the Bible,

"And again I say unto you, It is easier for a camel to go through the eye of a needle, than for a rich man to enter into the kingdom of God." (Matthew, 19:24)

Now, the Almighty repeats in the Qur'an what He had revealed to Christ:

"To those who reject Our Signs and treat them with arrogance, no opening will there be of the gates of heavens, nor will they enter the Garden, until the camel can pass through the eye of the needle: such is Our reward for those in sin." (7:40)

It revolves on proofs and evidence: If a crime happens, like murder or theft, the inspector must establish the relation between the murderer and the murdered, then the murderer and the tool of murder, and then the murderer and the place of murder. Without such relations no evidence can be said to exist. Now the statement made by Jesus, and written down in the Qur'an, is a proof that Chapter Seven of the Qur'an had been revealed previously. This religion is one, inherited by one prophet after another, although people do not perceive that. It is my intention here to bring to light these facts. The Qur'an is full of examples and proofs, and so are the sayings of Christ and Moses, peace be on them. Abraham, peace be upon him, for example, was named Abram; then Allah changed his name to Abraham. Now if you browse through the Holy Qur'an, you find the name of Abraham (Ibrahim in Arabic) mentioned sixty nine times, twenty five of which the name is given as Abram, and the other forty four it is Abraham. But not to tire the reader with many examples, I will give my last example:

Now read the following verse from the Qur'an:

"We did indeed aforetime give the Book to Moses: be not then in doubt of meeting him: and we made it a guide to the Children of Israel." (32:23)

The question is how can Muhammad, peace be on him, meet Moses, peace be on him, when the latter had died more than a thousand and five hundred years before the latter's time? This question baffled Muslims for over twelve hundred years, until a commentator on the Qur'an, Muhammad bin Ali bin Muhammad Al-Shawkani, who died in Sanaa, Yemen, in 1250 A.H., said in his book, *Fath Al-Qadir*, that the Messenger Muhammd, peace be upon him, met Moses, peace be upon him, during the former's night journey to heaven. Well sir, you can easily mislead people who have no guidance from their Lord, but not those who know when the relevant chapter was revealed to the Messenger. In fact, some editions of the Qur'an provide the reader just at the start of the chapter with a note about the order of revelation of that chapter. And checking about the relevant chapter, *Al-Sajdah* in Arabic, you find that it was revealed several years after the mentioned journey.

How do you tell someone not to see a certain person when he visits France, while you know that the visit took place several years ago?

A believer realizes the value of good guidance after one was astray, the value of clear sight after blurred vision, the value of contentedness after doubt, and the value of being on the straight way. He also knows the value of prostrating oneself to Allah after one was in the abyss of enslavement to the *taghoots* of the earth, with all their petty and worthless purposes: those who hang around them are certainly cut off from the reality of religion or religious light.

There are five major sins which the Almighty Lord has listed and commanded men to shun them so that their sins might be forgiven them:
"If you eschew the most heinous of the things which you are forbidden to do, We shall remit you from your evil deeds." (4:31)

To keep clear of those five enormous sins is the core of religion; Allah had promise the Children of Israel:

"Enter the gate prostrate; We shall forgive you your sins." (7:161)

Now what does it mean when someone prostrates? A prostrate person has his forehead on the floor; he is not walking, sitting, standing, or lying. In the above verse, the *taghoot*-controlled scholars interpret 'prostrate' (*sujjadan* in Arabic) as meaning 'bowing down'; for they say, 'How can one enter the gate prostrate?'

Everybody of course knows that bowing is not prostrating; so what is prostrating? Where can we find its meaning in the Holy Qur'an?

We know in math that if we have: a = b
And it was know to us that a = c
Therefore we conclude that b = c.

From such reasoning we say:

When we are told that: if we eschew the most heinous sins, Allah will forgive us our sins;

And we are told that: if we enter the gate prostrate, Allah will forgive us our sins;

Then the result must be: to prostrate = eschewing the most heinous sins. And that is evident by applying a most simple mathematical rule, which is known to every little pupil. But it is not something that the *taghoot*-controlled scholars realize. So, let's remind again that the major sins are the five things mentioned in verse 33 of Chapter 7.

The major sins are definitely not to be found in the worthless writings of the *taghoot*-controlled scholars, which include things like maintaining good relations with family.

Because by the logic of the *taghoot*-controlled scholars, Abraham, Muhammad, and Moses, peace be on them, are now in Hell; because they cut off relations with the family: we know that Abraham abandoned his father, Muhammad abandoned his uncle Abu Lahab, and Moses announced his disavowing the Children of Israel; all that is commonly known.

That the nucleus well comprehends the significance of keeping clear of the major sins, to adhere to that in their life – that is submission indeed; it is the meaning of embracing Islam. That will take place after the nucleus has dismissed from his heart any affection for those who harbor enmity for Allah: that is the mark of his faith. After that a nucleus will embark on his way to piety, to be a friend of Allah; he realizes his piety through fulfilling the following five terms:

Not to associate anything with Allah
To keep clear of shameful acts
To keep clear of sins
To keep clear of aggressing against anyone without right
Not to invent falsehood with regard to Allah; not to say concerning Allah that which he does not know to be true.

Once an individual has submitted, i.e. embraced Islam, he moves on to being a believer; then he fulfills the conditions of piety. When he is pious, then he is a friend of Allah, that is, he is among those who will not take other than Allah for protector. To realize this last rank, he must observe the following (all quoted from the Qur'an):

1. Join not anything as equal with Allah
2. Be good to your parents
3. Kill not your children on a plea of want – We provide sustenance for you and for your children
4. Do not come near to shameful deeds, whether open or secret
5. Take not life, which Allah has made sacred, except by way of justice and law
6. Come not near to the orphan's property, except to improve it, until he attains the age of full strength
7. Give measure and weight with full justice – no burden do We place on any soul, but that which it can bear
   (So far, we have what is due to other people, and due to environment.)
8. Whenever you speak, speak justly even if a near relative is concerned
9. Fulfill the Covenant of Allah
10. Do not follow other ways than Allah's; do no scatter about
    (That is to say, all men in the world are one nation.)

The above ten things represent true religion, and the messengers of Allah explained and elaborated these points, adding other things that derive from the above. When Allah ordains, 'perform prayer', it is because prayer restrains from shameful and unjust deeds; fasting is enjoined on believes at specified times; regular charity is ordained to support the kingdom of Allah in the earth; pilgrimage to the House of Allah is for all people to witness things that are of benefit to them. To adhere to all the above is patience; and those who observe them are the patient: but about patience one may go to our discussion of the patient and the jihad doer.

Every week you watch on the TV screen some imposters marketing their juggling (no more than frauds who manipulate and twist the sayings of Jesus, peace be upon him): they claim that Jesus granted sight to those who had it not; but they hide what Christ, peace be upon him, said that he had come to take away the vision of the sighted (John, 9:39)

They again mislead men and misrepresent what Christ said when they claim that he was an angel of peace; but it was he who said, "Think not that I am come to send peace on earth: I came not to send peace, but a sword." (Matthew, 10:34) Those jugglers will have to meet that Day of which they were warned. Allah is never inattentive of what they do. He says in the Qur'an:
"We grant them respite that they may grow in their iniquity." (3:178)

On the other hand, pilgrimage is not, as the *taghoot*-controlled scholars claim, only for Muslims, but for all people, so that they may witness benefits for themselves: but if they deny faith, Allah does not stand in need of any of His creatures.

It was further said above that faith was shown in that you have no more affection for those who are hostile to Allah: it is then that faith is written on your heart; then also prayer is enjoined on believers at fixed times. It is for believers, to restrain them from shameful and unjust deeds, and from transgression. Prayer is not as the misleading scholars claim: it is to aid a believer in worship. See for instance how the True Lord addresses Moses, peace be upon him, as the Qur'an reports:
"Serve me and establish regular prayer for celebrating My praise." 20:14)

As you see, prayer is not worship in itself', but it aids one to worship. Now Islam means submission; the word *ummah* means people who live on the earth between two points in time; and mankind are distributed as *ummahs* along timeline – an *ummah* being the people who live from one point along that line until another point; and for each *ummah* there are a Scripture and prophets and messengers. There is a Covenant established between those prophets and the Creator that they do not sever that chain. That is religion, and every time something happens on earth some revelation comes down from heaven concerning what is new. That is why we have this verse:

"Never comes anything to them of a renewed Message from their Lord, but they listen to it as in jest – their hearts toying as with trifles." (21:2-3)

Let's look at two other verses:

"O mankind! Fear you Lord! for the convulsion of the Hour of Judgment will be a thing terrible! The Day you shall see it, every mother giving suck shall forget her suckling-babe, and every pregnant female shall drop her load unformed: you shall see mankind as in a drunken riot, yet not drunk: but dreadful will be the Wrath of Allah." (22:1-2)

And now compare the above with what Christ, peace be upon him, said:

"But woe to them that are with child, and to them that give suck in those days." (Mark, 13:17)

CHAPTER THIRTY THREE

Sins

Man's deeds range between two poles, goodness and piety on one side; and sin and transgression on the other. We have said enough about goodness and piety before: so let's now shed some light on the long chain leading to sin. The first step is an inclination away from goodness, because of a certain flaw. More intensive is an intentional leaning away from goodness, with some transgression, injustice, and carelessness about the rights of others; it involves some confusion of truth with falsehood. This is sin, and it is a major fault which has been forbidden by Allah, and it increases in intensity along a long ladder of wrongdoing. One verse which helps us imagine this variation is the following:

"But if any is forced by hunger, with no inclination to transgression, Allah is indeed Oft-forgiving, Most Merciful." (5:3)

The actual situation of earning sin can be called 'committing', 'disobedience', 'fabrication of lies', 'oppression', 'transgression', 'intentional rejection of truth', 'disbelief', 'aggression', or 'treason'; and all of these fall under the general term of 'sin', each representing a grade or stage. Hence some of the above are called a 'heinous sin', as may be seen in the following verse of the Qur'an:

"Allah does not forgive that partners should be set up with Him; but He forgives anything else, to whom He pleases; to set

up partners with Allah is to devise a sin most heinous indeed."
(4:48)

That is the worst type of sin ever, though people are unmindful
of this fact. For more about this, one may refer to the chapter
about idolatry and idolaters, for there one may conceive the
importance of that in the general conception of religion.

The Almighty Lord mentions also sin when it is 'manifest sin',
and that is linked to fabricating lies against Allah (the reader may
have another look at the topic of the inventor of lies above.) Let's
recite His words in the Qur'an:
"Behold! How they invent a lie against Allah! But that by
itself is a manifest sin!" (4:50)

A believer, as the Almighty warns, must fulfill a pledge once
he has committed himself to it. Here are His words:
"O you who believe! You are forbidden to inherit women
against their will. Nor should you treat them with harshness,
that you may take away part of the dower you have given them
– except where they have been guilty of open lewdness; on the
contrary live with them on a footing of kindness and equity. If
you take a dislike to them it may be that you dislike a thing, and
Allah brings about through it a great deal of good. But if you
decide to take one wife in place of another, even if you had given
the latter a whole treasure for dower, take not the least bit of it
back: would you take it by slander and a manifest wrong? And
how could you take it when you have gone in unto each other,
and they have taken from you a solemn covenant?" (4:19-21)

Also we find elsewhere in the Qur'an:
"And those who malign believing men and women
undeservedly, bear on themselves a calumny and a glaring sin."
(33:58)

Elsewhere in the Qur'an, the Lord says:
"But if any one earns a fault or a sin and throws it on to one who is innocent, he carries on himself both a falsehood and a flagrant sin." (4:112)

As for enormous sins, the Almighty says:
"They ask you concerning wine and gambling. Say: 'In them is great sin, and some profit, for men; but the sin is greater than the profit.'" (2:218)

He warns elsewhere that when giving one's judgment concerning issues, one needs to be careful and to investigate well:
"O you who believe! Avoid suspicion as much as possible: for suspicion in some cases is a sin." (49:12)

Two sins mentioned in the Qur'an are expelling people out of their homes and eating up their money wrongfully. Let's read the relevant verse:
"And do not eat up your property among yourselves for vanities, nor use it as bait for the judges, with intent that you may eat up wrongfully and knowingly a little of other people's property." (2:188)

In brief, to do what Allah has banned, or to fail to do what He commands is a sin. For instance, it is a sin to conceal evidence.

Anyone who commits a sin, commits it only against himself.
Sinners are not to be considered the same degree of committing enormity, as we have said above: There are the habitually-disbelieving sinner; the hinderer of the good, transgressor, sinner; the lie-invening sinner; the transgressing sinner; the betraying sinner. It is a believer's first duty, the Almighty says, that he keeps clear of the above great sins:

"He rewards those who do evil, according to their deeds, and He rewards those who do good, with what is best. Those avoid great sins and shameful deeds, only falling into small faults – verily your Lord is ample in forgiveness." (53:31-32)

The point to remember most is that sin should be conceived in accordance with its conditions laid down by Allah: we may not add to those conditions, and we may not take away any of them – for if we do we would be fabricating lies against Allah, and those who fabricate lies against Allah will never prosper.

REFERENCES

1. *The Qur'an*

2. *The Bible: King James Version*, Christ's words in red. Holman Bible Publishers, Tn; Eyre and Spottiswoode (Publishers), London.

3. *Al-Munjed fi Llughah*, Pub. Dar al-Mashreq; dist. Al-Maktabah al-Sahrqiyah; 2nd ed. 1987.

4. *Random House Dictionary*; S.E.; 1987

5. Anderson, *The Production Pattern (Asia)*

6. Will Durant, *Story of Civilization*; Pub. Simon and Schuster, 1963.

7. Abdul Fattah Imam, *The Despot* (in Arabic); Alam Al-Ma'rifah

8. Muhammad Mutawalli al-Sha'rawee, *This Is Islam*; Pub. Dar al-Kutub al-Misriyah, and Dar al-Hurriyah, Cairo, Egypt.

9. Jawdat Sa'eed, *Work: [A Composite of] Ability and Will*; Dar al-Fikr al-Mu'aser; Beirut, Lebanon.

10. Jalalu-d-Din 'Abdul-Rahman al-Suyuti, *Al-Itqan fi 'ulum al-Qur'an*; pub. Al-Ma'rifah Publishing House, Beirut, Lebanon.

11. Ibn al-Muqaffa', Al-Adab al-Sagheer

12. Ali al-Nuri al-Safaqisi, *Siraj al-Qari' al-Mubtaddi' wa Ghaith al-Naf' fi al-Qira'at al-Sab'*; Mustafa al-Halabi Press

13. Muhammad al-Sayyid al-Dawoodi, *Min Kunuz al-Qur'an*, Dar al-Mu'arif

14. Abu Abdullah Muhammad, s/o Muhammad, s/o Dawood al-Sihajee '*Ajroomiyah*'; Pub: Mustafa al-Babee al-Halabee Bookstore, Cairo

15. Al-Tabarani, *Al-Mu'jam al-Kabir*, Vol. 8, p.282

16. John Locke *On Civil Rule*: [My reference is a translation of this book into Arabic by Majed Fakhri,] published in Beirut, 1959

ABOUT THE AUTHOR

Born in the village of Kuneitra in the Golan Heights on Feb 28, 1947, Anor Azhak's early years were spent in his grandmother's village nearby, where religion played an important part in his everyday life. His family moved to Damascus when he was a young boy. There, his performance in school was erratic, sometimes top and sometimes bottom of the class. Even then, religion held his interest and attention, as he would spend days in places of worship. He was full of questions but he did not find many answers that made much sense. In retrospect, his deep desire to find these answers has been the main force shaping his life.

He emigrated to the U.S. at the age of eighteen to avoid being drafted into the army, which conflicted with one of the many beliefs he still holds. Unfortunately, moving away put great strains on his potential to obtain a formal college education that he felt very capable of accomplishing. Because he did not have a degree from a recognized institution, his quest for answers was hindered. In the land of opportunity, he had to work hard to earn a living. Fortunately, after twenty years of hard work in the construction business, he was able to retire at the age of forty and devote all of his time his books.

His journey to find the truth began nearly thirty-three years ago. It began merely by gathering thoughts and putting them on paper. Added to endless nights of reading, research and investigation, he began to see a purpose and felt the obligation to continue what he had begun. He visited and discussed his ideas with scholars all over the world, only to find that most were opposed to his non-mainstream ideas. Yet, he has not met with any scholar who has been able to prove his research wrong. Fortunately, some scholars responded well to his research and are anxiously waiting to see what his research and studies have shown. Gradually, he began to find answers to those questions that have always puzzled him. Christ said, "The truth will set you free." He wishes to share these truths he has found with everyone so that they may be set free. This is the motivation for writing his book.